A
Rush
to Judgment

A Journey with Trump, God, and Love

SID BOWDIDGE

PAGE PUBLISHING, INC.
New York, NY

First originally published by Page Publishing, Inc. 2018

ISBN 978-1-64298-429-3 (Paperback)
ISBN 978-1-64298-442-2 (Hardcover)
ISBN 978-1-64298-430-9 (Digital)

Printed in the United States of America

ACKNOWLEDGMENTS

S pecial thanks to Denise. If not for you and your love, this story never happens.

Thank you to my best friend Jason Squeglia. With your support, we made a difference and enjoyed a thrill ride of a lifetime together.

To my other close friends and allies, Charles, Robert, Matt, Andrew, Stuart, Suzie, Elias, and Amanda, to name just a few, thank you for all you did to help Make America Great Again.

Last but certainly not least, thank you to the thousands of volunteers across the country who, without your assistance, our victory couldn't have come.

CHAPTER 1

Raised without Faith

S toneham, Massachusetts, in a time when everyone knew the police officers and riding the bumper of the town bus in a snowstorm would not get you killed. I was the oldest of four children and was blessed to have had hardworking parents who provided the necessities of life. The only thing missing was my father; he worked day and night. Unfortunately, part of the reason for that was it kept him away from being intimately involved with the family. The repercussions of which were the arguments that my parents would have nearly every night. Terrible arguments at the dinner table which made for an uneasy and fearful life as a child growing up. Religion was not part of our lives so there was no outlet nor anyone to talk with, even in a spiritual sense. God did not exist in our house growing up. My grandparents on my father's side were Christians. They were members of their local church and always attended. Their relationship with the Lord was a big part of their life and they were very happy. Unfortunately, that didn't transcend to their only son, my father. On my mother's side, the only time God was mentioned was in the context of swearing.

Things were so contentious between my parents that at thirteen I ran away from home for a week. There were other times as well but I was always found around town somewhere. Grounded over and over for weeks at a time became the norm for my teenage life. At sixteen and a half, I ran away for another week, sleeping in my car every night and chased by my father three times. I managed to outpace him each time, as I would drive through stop signs and traffic lights to get away. In the summer of 1972, at sixteen, I was being left home alone every weekend as my father would head up to the family summer home on Long Island, Maine. I started smoking pot, and shortly after that, began taking a variety of pills to ease my troubled life at home. I was always a hard worker and had begun working when I was twelve years old. I had a paper route, then washing dishes at the town bakery at fourteen. I worked at Jack in the Box at sixteen, and then at a machine shop after school at seventeen. It was here on January 17, 1974, where things took a turn for the worse. During afternoon breaks, a friend and I would go out and get high on marijuana.

Shortly before five o'clock and near the end of this day, I was operating a milling machine and cutting half-inch depths into cast iron centers. I was hurrying to finish when a fellow worker came over to me and asked me a question. Back then, OSHA (Occupational Safety and Health Administration) had not yet mandated that machines have two buttons in order to begin their operation. Hitting the single big red button would begin the cutting process. The cast iron centers needed to be tightened into a vice directly under a spinning half-inch blade. My coworker stepped over to the right front of my machine. I looked up as I inadvertently hit the red button which then dropped the blade down to do its cutting process. My right hand was still under the blade. I didn't move it out in time. The blade cut down through the back of my hand and nearly through my palm. I screamed but couldn't pull my hand out. It was too late. I had to wait until the preset cutting depth was reached, at which point, the blade lifted up automatically. I pulled my hand out, my middle finger swinging by a small piece of skin. My last two fingers were still attached but the entire back of my hand was hanging over. In shock and bleeding profusely, I walked into the foreman's office. I sat down in a chair while a very courageous engineer came into the office and knelt in front of me, holding my hand together as best he could while waiting for the ambulance. Over the next few years and five operations, I was left with two plastic knuckles, a shortened middle finger, and a lot of scars. Through the grace of God, I did not lose all my fingers.

My operations were all performed at Massachusetts General Hospital. After the first operation, I recall being on a floor with amputees. This was clearly God making sure I didn't feel sorry for myself. There were patients there of all ages, some were missing legs and arms. I soon realized how very fortunate I was. Speaking of The Man above, he wasn't mentioned much in our house growing up. We never went to church, and my only experience involving God was going to Sunday school a couple of times with a friend. I found it to be so foreign that I snuck out a back door and walked home. Nobody cared, and my life going forward was godless. My parents divorced when I was eighteen after years of constant arguing and fighting over everything. My relationship with my father became worse after he moved out, and I lived with my mother and my three younger siblings. I tried to protect my mother one time when my father came to the house and remember being slammed up against the wall by him. As a teenager, I hated my father so much I even loosened the lug nuts on his truck in the middle of the night with one hand and a half, no less. Fortunately, nothing disastrous happened. No kid should have to feel so much hatred.

I was never much of a drinker, so I self-medicated for years. Unlike modern times, there wasn't much concern given when doctors prescribed pain medication in the seventies and eighties. I was prescribed countless bottles and refills of pain medication upon each operation. What followed was years of smoking pot, snorting cocaine, and taking pills of different varieties. Somehow, through this, I managed to start a family and get married at nineteen years old, always holding a job. There was a girl who worked in the office of the machine shop where I was injured. Her name was Lynne and we fell in love. My daughter Kerry was born in 1976, and my son Brandon in 1981. Brandon had spinal meningitis at seven months old and came eight hours away from dying from it. If it weren't for the good Lord and the Children's Hospital in Boston, he wouldn't be here today. They told us *if* he survives, the disease, along with the experimental antibiotics, would likely leave him blind, deaf, mentally retarded, or physically handicapped. We signed our lives away and hoped for the best. Of course, today I know God played a role in this and it wasn't Brandon's time, and he survived.

Three weeks later, while still in Children's Hospital, we realized that he couldn't hear us as we were calling his name one day. An infant hearing exam was ordered for the next day. I'll never forget going into Boston by myself and being told that he was profoundly deaf. I sat in my car, devastated but thankful he was still with us. Lynne and I began taking sign language classes when he was an infant. We always communicated with him in signed English rather than American Sign Language (ASL). We rarely allowed him to lean on his affliction and encouraged him he could do anything he wanted, regardless. He played on the town little league team when he was an adolescent, and I coached so that I'd be able to sign to him during the game. Both of my children grew up to be terrifically inspiring and productive adults. Kerry is an RN and lives in New Hampshire along with her husband and our grandson Caleb. Brandon is the Auto Tech Instructor at the California School for the Deaf in Riverside, California. Both of my kids were not raised with faith—one of my biggest regrets. I was a good father, always had a job, and supported my family. I also was a good husband in the sense that I wasn't abusive, never drank much, and was always around. However, I wasn't always faithful, and in that sense, failed my wife, my children, and my marriage.

CHAPTER 2

Always Behind the Eight Ball

Lynne and I had a good relationship, had lots of friends, and did everything together. But something was missing and I could never figure it out. At forty years old, I decided the grass must be greener on the other side, found a girlfriend, and filed for a divorce after twenty years. Lynne and I first dated when I was sixteen and she was fifteen. She was a great wife and a great mother. We had a good relationship, owned a home in Burlington, Massachusetts, and things were pretty good. But without the Lord's moral compass, I set my own guidelines of how I'd run my life. After all, it was my life, right? It was easy to blame everyone else for the injustices I perceived. I could justify all of my actions, no matter who I might be hurting. I was such a jerk, and leaving was so unfair to my family. So many people think they have it together and think they know what's important in their lives. I was one of them but I still had so much to learn.

When I left, my kids were twenty and fifteen years old. Kerry moved out on her own shortly thereafter, and Brandon moved in with me after about six months. The divorce hurt them all terribly and I will always regret what I did. I started into another relationship with what would become my second marriage with my wife Marie. We dated for a while and I moved in with her and her two kids after about a year, and then moved out six months later. From there, we were on and off for nine long years, finally getting married in the tenth year of being together. The reasons involving our breakups were rarely my fault, of course, tongue in cheek here. I would stack the deck, adding up all of the injustices as I saw them. Here I was again, justifying how righteous I was. It was during this relationship that I first delved into therapy. Shortly after I met Marie, she informed me she was seeing a therapist, asking me if I would consider checking it out for my own well-being. My first thought was, *Wouldn't you know it? I hooked up with a loony tune.* I actually believed that if you were seeing a therapist then, you must be nuts to some degree. Boy, did I have a lot to learn!

I agreed to go and found therapy to be exceptionally rewarding. Any health insurance coverage, at best, only covered about a dozen visits but I went for years. I didn't mind paying for it out of my own pocket as I was discovering things about myself and making positive changes. Although I found therapy to be exceptionally rewarding, it ultimately didn't *fix* my relationship. I did learn a lot about myself and why I did the things I did, why I reacted to certain things in certain ways, such as realizing that my righteous behavior was a reflection of my father. My dad's way was always the right way, and ultimately, the only way. My personality mirrored my father in so many ways. It had a negative impact on all relationships in my life, friends included. I came to find and believe that our personalities are developed during our childhood. How we're treated and what we see growing up will reflect immensely on how we treat others and how we react to things as adults. All of this behavior had a negative effect on me financially, as well. Although I was always employed, I also seemed able to spend everything I made. Basically, my life seemed to be organized chaos. Marie had her issues and baggage, as well, and I had no tolerance for it. Our relationship was emotional turmoil. Within the first year of my marriage, I left and filed for divorce. Without faith, I was my own guiding light and I was always behind the eight ball. Houston, we have a problem.

CHAPTER 3

Marriage Number 3—God's Not Dead

After a couple of girlfriends, which didn't work out ultimately for all the same reasons as my marriages, I met Denise. We met online and began talking on the phone for a couple of weeks. I found her to be incredibly warm, funny, and genuine, finally meeting her for our first date on September 28, 2008. I'll never forget when we first met. We got out of our cars next to each other and proclaimed, "It's you!" She had the most inviting smile I've ever seen. To this day, her smile can change my mood instantly. We fell in love, and even though we lived eighty miles away from each other, it didn't keep us apart. I put thousands of miles on my car in a few short months. At that time, I lived in Peabody, Massachusetts, and she lived in Southbridge, Massachusetts, a long way apart. I couldn't be with her enough. She was vibrant, smart, funny, warm, loving, caring, and giving. I proposed to her in December of the same year to which she accepted. Several months later, we decided to move in together and moved to Bedford, New Hampshire. Her youngest daughter Sara had decided to go to the University of Southern New Hampshire and off we went.

Our wedding date was set for July 18, 2009, in York, Maine. We both love the ocean as well as the mountains, so New Hampshire was perfect for us. At last, away from all the hustle and bustle of Massachusetts, we loved it. Not to mention getting away from Massachusetts politics as far left as you can get. Shortly before our wedding day, we set off for York, Maine, to acquire our wedding license. We argued and fought nearly the whole time going there. Things had calmed down and we went through with it after all. Everything was fantastic for the first several months, and then I began doing what I'd done through all of my relationships. I began stacking the deck of all the things I didn't like. Before I knew it, we separated and I moved out, leaving the poor woman on her own with her teenage daughter. However, the love we felt for each other was so strong that we didn't want to be apart and we'd move back in. Only to do the same routine two or three more times over the next five years.

Denise had always been a spiritual woman, but no matter how hard she tried, it wasn't for me. Oh, I tried it—going to church with her on several occasions and enjoying the time I spent. We joined a nondenominational church in Concord, New Hampshire. I even went so far as to get baptized but not for the right reason. I realized later that I was doing it for her, and as you might imagine, it didn't last long. We had gone to church for several months but got divorced during the winter of 2014, but continued to date. It was looking as though this was going to be the final end to our relationship. Denise stayed over my place one night, and in the morning, I asked her about a particular screwdriver I was missing. She mentioned she had it in her trunk and that it was hers. I began telling her it was not hers and why that damn screwdriver was so important to me. I made such a big deal out of it that she soon was in tears, telling me she'd give it back. It was now April 2015. We stopped seeing each completely, and for the first time since 2008, she was out of my life. She stopped coming back as she always had. She'd had enough.

My father passed away a month later on May 23, 2015. I sat in my apartment alone and began reflecting back on my life. I had just turned fifty-nine years old in April, and I felt I had nothing. Not many friends, not many close relatives, not many people who cared a lot. It's interesting how the death of a parent can wake you up and make you reflect on your life. Where had my life gone? How did it go so fast? How could I be so alone? After all, it wasn't as though I was a bad person. I helped people whenever I could and never broke the law. I had been a good father for the most part. One particular day soon after my father died, I opened my trunk and looked at a small plastic toolbox which had just the necessities. Thinking about what a jerk I'd been to Denise around the screwdriver, I left this toolbox by the back door where Denise was living. It was my olive branch. The next day, my phone rang and it was her. She'd heard that my father had passed and called to share her condolences and asked if I'd like some company. I was very grateful and expressed my appreciation. Shortly after she arrived, she told me she had a movie she'd like me to watch. I said "Sure, what is it?" "*God's Not Dead*," she replied, and I agreed to watch it. I never felt that I was an atheist but more of an agnostic, so I didn't object. This particular night and this particular movie changed my life for the rest of my days on this earth in a way I'd never imagined. God sent His Holy Spirit to save me, and saved I was.

I came to find out later, Denise had never stopped praying for me. Praying that somehow God would help change me. Help me see my ways, and He did. There are many parts in this movie which are so profound, especially if you have an open mind and heart. The premise for the movie is based around a college student signing up for a philosophy class. He's warned by another student during sign-up that the professor is very difficult. Not sure what that meant, he takes this class anyway. On the first day, he finds out the professor is a devout atheist. His first instructions to the class are that everyone write on a piece of paper *God is dead.* The student, being a Christian, refuses to write this and is challenged by the professor. In turn, he gives him the option of proving that God exists, otherwise he will fail him. In his attempt to prove God exists, he points out that a philosopher from ancient times once said, "Without God, everything is permissible." This sentence hit me like a ton of bricks. I suddenly realized this was the way I'd gone about my life. Another statement he made was, "Our moral compass is a direct line to God." Something in me immediately began to change. I felt coolness throughout my body and goosebumps came over me. I even shivered and had a feeling I cannot describe. I would later realize the Holy Spirit had just entered my body. A tear ran down my cheek as I became very aware I had been justifying everything I did in my life. All the hurt I had caused was because without God in my life everything was permissible! I simply justified it.

During another important part of the movie, the student strongly says to the atheist professor, "Why do you hate God?" The professor replies back in anger, "Because He took everything away from me!" The student softly responds, "How can you hate something if it doesn't exist?" I sat watching with tears running down my cheeks. Poignantly, the student describes that it's a choice. God wants us to have a choice. Believe or not believe, it's up to you, He doesn't force us. The students one by one stand and proclaim, "God's not dead." I sat there sobbing, and I knew I had made my decision. For the very first time in my life, I believed that God does in fact exist. The reason I know? Because from that night on, I've never been the same person. From that point on, I've walked with the Lord in my heart, and it has changed me dramatically and made everything in my life better. Most importantly, me. I began to love unconditionally for the first time in my life, just as He loves us unconditionally.

Denise knew what was happening and hugged me while we cried together. I was so sorry for how I'd hurt her. We began going back to church where, soon after, she herself baptized me—for the right reason this time. God changed my heart that night and humbled me. Both of us having a strong relationship with God has brought us closer than I ever could have envisioned. We're now going on three years since that night, and we have been graced by the good Lord more times than I can count. From that moment and forever, I love Denise for her differences. How I wish I was raised having a relationship with the Lord, for I now know my life would have been much more peaceful. Denise's prayers paid off, and God worked through her. I finally became aware that my problem was never with my marriages, my problem was with God. You see, it is a choice. A choice that God waits for you to make. The invitation is there for everyone. Once you do and accept Him as your savior, the rewards are plenty. You simply need to keep your eyes and heart open, and watch what He will do next in your life. I once heard *what the Holy Spirit touches, the Holy Spirit changes.* It's never too late.

CHAPTER 4

"Hey, Honey, Trump's Coming to Town!"

It was June 2015, when Donald Trump was making his second visit to New Hampshire as a presidential candidate. Denise had followed Trump since back in the eighties and had read his book, *Art of the Deal*. Together, we had enjoyed the hit show *The Apprentice* for years. So when Denise one day said, "Hey, honey, Trump's coming to town, want to go see him?" I was all in. We went to a large gathering at a home in our town of Bedford. It was there that we changed from celebrity viewing to realizing we were very interested in Trump's policies of change for America. The media was there, and I was interviewed at the end of this event by NBC's Katie Tur who asked me what I liked about Trump. I told her that number one, I liked that he wasn't a politician. Along with that, I believed he was a man who would stand up for the middle class and not lay down to special interest groups, and stand up for what was best for our country, bringing jobs back and keep companies doing business here, such as the Ford plant being built in Mexico. After my response, she uttered under her breath "Why am I not surprised?" as she walked away. This was my first experience with how nasty the liberal media was to become in their hate for Trump and his supporters. Denise and I loved Trump's bravado regarding America First, stopping illegal immigration, and fixing the Veteran's Administration. We had watched Obama dismantle this country piece by piece over eight long years. I recall coming away from this event feeling something I hadn't felt in a long time—pride. America's interests first? What a novel idea!

There were only a few of Trump's New Hampshire staff hired at this point and they were all there. As I would learn, their job was to pull us in as volunteers. They took our names and phone numbers, asking us to come in and help. The next day, Denise asked me to go with her to the Manchester campaign office to do phone banking. I had never volunteered before and phone banking wasn't at the top of my list of things I wanted to do. Well, she was going without me so reluctantly I agreed, and phone banking I went, again and again. We got to know the staff well. State Director Matt Ciepielowski, Deputy State Director Andrew Georgevits, and staffer Zac Montanaro were terrific people. In the early months of the campaign, Mr. Trump was coming to New Hampshire twice a week at times. New Hampshire is the second state in the country to vote in the primary, and therefore very important to all the candidates. The staff quickly recognized our commitment to the cause and began asking us to do more. We began setting up at Trump rallies. This meant being there several hours before Mr. Trump's arrival and a few hours after his departure. It was fun being part of each exciting event as the energy level inside the venues was like being at a rock concert and we loved every minute of it.

A few months before this, I had quit my sales job and had decided to try something completely different—being a masseuse. I liked being self-employed and began looking at massage training. Denise was already self-employed doing some real estate work.

Deputy State Director Andrew Georgevits was responsible for these events, and quite often, my task was to assist Andrew in handling the logistics of the event. At the end of an early on event in Laconia, NH, I asked Andrew if they had any staff openings. I'll always remember his answer, "This is a young man's game, Sid, you don't want to do this." I had been working out for the past twenty-five years and was in better shape than most guys half my age, and quite frankly, every one of them as well. Nevertheless, I was still interested in a more responsible role in helping to get Mr. Trump into office. As the events continued one after another, I sometimes handled security near the stage to make sure there were no whack jobs getting near Mr. Trump. Suit and tie was the attire. Toward the end of the summer of 2015, I was being asked to drive a staff car in Mr. Trump's motorcade when he would come into the state. This was becoming a job for Denise and me, and we were committing more and more time to it. We loved being a part of such a cause and couldn't get enough. We began living off our savings so we could volunteer as much as possible. This was more important than anything either of us had ever done. Our conservative way of life was being threatened. We began to realize that if Trump didn't win the presidency, our country would fall into the socialist abyss to which Obama had orchestrated so well.

Secret Service was not yet involved, so I got to know Mr. Trump's personal security staff well—Keith Schiller, Trump's personal security guard, and half a dozen others. They were all great people and extremely dedicated. At one event, I was handed a challenge coin from Keith. It had the Trump family crest on it and is quite an honor to receive one. A challenge coin is a small coin or medallion (usually military) bearing an organization's insignia or emblem and carried by the organization's members. In the military, these coins are presented by unit commanders in recognition of special achievement by a member of the unit. Outside of the military, they're also given as rewards or awards for outstanding service or performance of duty. Keith was a longtime New York City detective and one tough son of a bitch. I was honored that he recognized my dedication. Denise and I most often worked these events together. We both fully believed in Mr. Trump's agenda to put America's interests first. We also felt strongly that the last eight years of the Obama administration had taken us to the brink of no return in terms of ruining our country. It was during this time that I realized how the Lord was working in our lives. We were closer than we'd felt in years. It seemed as though I was looking at life through a different set of glasses. We were making new friends and thankful for every day. We also began to believe, over time, that divine intervention was taking place.

One time during the summer of 2015, we were interviewed after an event by a reporter from Lifezette, Laura Ingram's website. She asked us what we liked about Trump and also what we did for a living. I replied that my background was sales and marketing but that I was delving into massage therapy. This article was published and could be found on Google. Little did I know what a prominent role this article would play in my life down the road. As we continued working the rallies, we found at least one liberal nutjob at every event. In the early months, there was a younger guy who had a scraggly beard and a Lincoln top hat who would show up at the events. He was your classic hippie type and would always have a handful of wildflowers he'd try to hand Mr. Trump as he was walking out after the rally. I was driving in the motorcade for an event in Atkinson, New Hampshire, near the end of the summer of 2015. *Flowers*, a nickname we gave this guy, showed up again. From my Suburban, I instructed one of our volunteers to escort him to the outskirts of the parking lot. The event ended, and the motorcade began leaving. I happened to have three of Mr. Trump's security team in my staff vehicle. As it just so happened, *Flowers* was standing on the corner. As the motorcade drove past him and my SUV approached him, two of the guys put their windows down and yelled, "Get a job, *!#*!#*!" It was one of the funnier moments when driving which otherwise was a very serious job.

It was such a privilege being selected to drive in these motorcades. I got to know Michael Glassner, Trump's political director, as well as Corey Lewandowski, Trump's campaign manager, along with the entire team around Mr. Trump. If you were selected to drive, the protocol was you had to be at the airport two hours before Mr. Trump landed. At this point in the campaign, only the New Hampshire State Police and locals were involved for protection. Nonetheless, a bomb sweep had to be done on all vehicles by a bomb-sniffing dog. Each vehicle had to have all doors opened along with hood and tailgate. Fifteen minutes before *wheels down*, we'd all pull out onto the tarmac and line up. Mr. Trump's Boeing 757 would land, taxi over to us, and we'd then pull up alongside the plane. There were always two Suburbans with five SWAT Team State Police in the motorcade, armed with M-16 machine guns and ready for anything. The entourage came out of the plane and down the stairs. They all knew ahead of time which vehicle they were to get in to. When Mr. Trump got in the front vehicle, the motorcade departed and you'd better be ready to go. Escorted by police, I found it difficult not going for the brakes when approaching red lights as we sped through them. You had to focus on the rear of the vehicle in front of you, trying to stay the same speed but also not getting too close and not too far away. You also had to be aware of not allowing a car into the motorcade between the vehicles. More than once, some idiot would try, oblivious that they were pulling in between a police motorcade. Within a few seconds, one of the State Police would come up from behind, siren blaring, and pull them over. I always hoped they got a ticket.

Another arrival into NH Summer 2015

Bedford NH June 2015

Bedford NH. Denise ready to say hello to Mr. Trump

Denise and I early on. July 4th parade
in Freedon NH July 4th 2015

Denise with Ivanka July 2015

I could never get enough of this big bird coming in

Ivanka came to the Manchester NH HQ July 2015

(left to right) Staffer Zach Montanaro,
NH State Rep. Fred Doucette and
Trump State Director Matt Ciepielowski

Mr Trump at the Concord NH State House to
deliver his check and officially entering the race
in NH. I found myself on TV the next day

Mr Trump's Boeing 757 was in for service. He
arrived into Nashua NH Municipal Airport.
We picked him up in his Citation

Mr. Trump leaving NH Summer 2015

One of many trips into NH through the Primary

Where it all began Bedford NH. Deputy State
Director Andrew Georgevits making sure Denise
doesn't get too close to Mr. Trump

CHAPTER 5

We Answer the Call to Serve

By the end of September 2015, it was being discussed to open a campaign office in Keene, New Hampshire. I threw my hat in the ring to be the manager and was finally hired on staff. We needed a field rep to handle the western part of the state, and the campaign hired both of us. Denise, being hired to fill that role, was recognized for the diligence she'd shown as a volunteer. Mind you, Keene is the liberal hotbed of the state so we had our work cut out for us. More and more, we began to see how the good Lord was working in our lives. It just kept getting better and better, and we were very grateful and humbled. On October 1, I began running the Keene campaign office. We were officially on Trump's staff and proud of it. The money wasn't great at $2,500/month, but we weren't doing it for the money. We began driving to and from Keene every day, seven days a week. Unfortunately, and unknown to us, the office had no heat and the rooftop unit was broken. As we headed into late October and then November, we found ourselves freezing while we were there. The landlord was a Trump supporter and kept telling us he was having it repaired. But there was always another reason why it was delayed, and we spent many a cold day into the evening, freezing our butts off. We tried space heaters but they could only do so much. Nonetheless, we had supporters and volunteers pouring through the door day and night. We had a job to do and a country to save, and nothing was going to keep us from succeeding. Even in Keene, there were thousands of people who loved Trump. It was very common to have someone come in for a Trump sign or information and tell us that they had been a Democrat all their life but they were voting for Trump. Another common statement we heard was, they voted for Obama, which was a mistake, but were going to vote for Trump this time. We were off and running.

When I wasn't driving in the motorcade, I'd be working a rally and the common theme was huge crowds and long lines to get in. Denise and I had never been involved in politics before and we were gradually finding out that this not the norm. People of every walk of life were attending and wanting to volunteer to help out. They all said the same thing: we're sick and tired of struggling and watching this country go down the tube. They often talked of all the businesses in the area which had closed up and left, or downsized. We shared their struggles. No matter how hard we worked, it seemed we never got ahead. Higher expenses on utilities, food, and in essence, everything had been climbing in price for years, except our paychecks. No one will ever convince me that Obama didn't have an agenda to take this country down and out. The progressive movement had been growing in this country since the early nineteen hundreds, welfare being the first handout by the liberal left. And it was getting worse decade by decade. I truly believe Obama was groomed to put the finishing touches on making us a socialist country. The PC culture had grown from the progressive movement, along with the ACLU, a horrible organization. Our country was being taken away from us, away from conservative minded citizens. Whether it was Hillary or Bernie, either one would've been the icing on the cake. The abyss of socialism was just around the corner, and we'd be damned if we were going sit back and let that happen. In the Keene office, we handed out thousands of yard signs as well as four-by-eight signs to supporters. At times, as fast as we'd hand them out and people would put them up, they'd be stolen or destroyed. It's interesting how people, who propose to be so tolerant and accepting of everyone, can't tolerate someone having a difference of opinion. We never knew one single conservative that had taken down a Hillary or Bernie sign.

Michael Savage was correct in the title of his first book, *Liberalism is a Mental Disorder.*

October 16, 2015, Mr. Trump came to Tyngsboro, Massachusetts. I was asked to drive in the motorcade, and Denise was working the event. We had hired a part-time person to help cover the office. The rally was being held in the gymnasium at an elementary school similar to other events, with a full house as usual. When I arrived at the Nashua New Hampshire airport, there were seventeen police officers on motorcycles and the usual State and local police vehicles. There were two black Chevrolet Suburbans left there by the advance team for us as staff cars. At this point, Mr. Trump's life had been threatened enough that Secret Service had been ordered to protect him. After proper check-in with them and the usual vehicle bomb sweep was completed, all vehicles were set in a particular order. A couple of hours later, Mr. Trump landed in his Cessna Citation X private jet which had the Trump crest emboldened on the fuselage right behind the front cabin windows. A beautiful ten-passenger jet plane which can cruise at an altitude of 51,000 feet and 604 mph maximum speed. His Boeing 757 was in for service which took nearly a month to complete. Mr. Trump and his entourage got in the vehicles, and off to Tyngsboro we went. It was an incredible sight and extremely exciting to drive down the highway with nine motorcycle police leading the motorcade, along with eight more bringing up the rear. There were six vehicles in between. All of the blue lights made it very difficult to concentrate later on the return trip back to Nashua in the dark.

It was a typical Trump event—a mob scene. People were walking to the school from all over, parking where they could find space. As the motorcade approached the proximity of the school, people on both sides of the road stopped to wave flags and signs. There were hundreds of people outside who couldn't get in. We pulled up in front of the school and waited. You could not leave the vehicle in case of an emergency departure. And in Trump fashion, at the end of the event, he came outside and walked the entire barrier shaking hands, talking to people, and signing autographs. He loved the people and he loved the crowds. He loved America, and people felt it. I often heard him say to the crowd, "I have a wonderful family and a successful business. I don't need to do this, folks. The only reason I'm doing this is I can't stand to sit and watch what's being done to this great country." We and everyone else believed him. The event ended, and the motorcade sped away from the school. People were everywhere, lined up on both sides of the streets continuing to wave flags and signs. We brought Mr. Trump back to his Citation and there, before he left, he made a point to have his picture taken with every single motorcycle officer next to his plane, shaking their hands and thanking them for their service. They loved him and couldn't get enough. Trump's popularity was incredible, and I had a firsthand view again and again. You could tell something special was happening in this country. People were feeling proud to be an American again. Denise and I began to believe wholeheartedly that Trump was going to be our next President of the United States. We believed this from the time we started and never wavered from this belief. As the officers got on their motorcycles and pulled away from the plane, Mr. Trump asked, "Where are my drivers?" He then walked over to the two of us, handed us each a fifty-dollar bill and shook my hand, thanking me for my service. You could've knocked me over with a feather. I thought to myself afterward, *Did that really just happen?* I can assure you, Hillary never did that.

Mr. Trump and his staff came back to New Hampshire for another rally shortly after. This is where the Lord began to bless me again with more good fortune. I was requested to drive in the motorcade again and there were to be two staff cars. Trump State Director Matt Ciepielowski informed me there was going to be a new driver that night—a gentleman by the name of Jason Squeglia. I came to find out Jason had been volunteering for the Massachusetts campaign staff for a while. He lived in Dunstable, Massachusetts, and occasionally would come up to help out in New Hampshire. We'd never met, and Matt asked me to call him to give him some details on the protocol of driving in the motorcade—things such as you don't talk unless someone's speaking to you, what you hear discussed in the vehicle is never to be repeated, stay focused on the bumper of the SUV in front of you, and don't get distracted. I brought Jason water and snacks as it's a long shift. From the time you arrive two hours before *wheels down* to the point of *wheels up* can be several hours. The motorcade does not depart until the wheels of that airplane are tucked underneath. Protection is required right up until that plane lifts off the ground.

I came to find out Jason didn't need much training. He had owned his own trucking business in the past and was a real pro. He *got it.* We hit it off right from the start and had lots of time to talk before Mr. Trump's arrival. We shared some of our experiences helping the campaign, as well as some of our life history. He currently owned his own environmental company in Massachusetts, and was beginning to dedicate more and more time to the campaign while his partner ran the business. In time, I came to see that we could always count on Jason to help out and be the consummate professional, not to mention one of the best people I'd met on the campaign. We brought the entourage back to the airport from the rally. It was dusk. The motorcade lined up; the vehicles side by side. At times, it can take about fifteen minutes for the jet engines to get ramped up and everyone inside the plane to get settled. We had our windows down and were talking to each other. Mr. Trump's Boeing 757 began to roll only about one hundred yards from where we sat. As the plane began to power up and turn away from us, we were pelted by a sand storm from the jet blast. The inside of both vehicles were covered in sand from the tarmac. It was in our hair, ears, all over our suits, and in every nook and cranny in the SUVs. We still laugh about it to this day. I didn't know it then, but the Lord was introducing me to my best friend. A friend that, as time went on, I grew to love. As the months wore on, Jason and I would share the experience of a lifetime.

Denise and I were holding Trump support meetings all over western New Hampshire, many at night and quite often driving the fifty miles home in snowstorms or staying at a hotel in Keene because it was too treacherous to drive home. This mission we were on brought us closer than ever. The Lord was using us as he needed—soldiers to help Him save this great country of ours. Don Jr. came to the Keene office during the primary. I wasn't there, but according to Denise, he was nothing but an incredibly nice guy, polite and respectful. Denise had arranged to have some supporters there, and Don talked about how much the family appreciated the support of New Hampshire. I found the same thing with Ivanka. I was driving one time when Mr. Trump was coming to a rally in Concord, New Hampshire. Unbeknownst to me, ahead of time, Ivanka and Jared got into the back seat of my Suburban upon pick up at the plane. While driving to the event, I had asked Ivanka if she'd mind signing Denise's book. I had Mr. Trump's latest book, *Crippled America*, on the console. Her response was that she'd be happy to, and so she did. Right before we departed the rally, I asked her if she wouldn't mind having her dad sign it as well. Political Director Michael Glassner was about to get in the vehicle and Ivanka asked him to take it to Mr. Trump to sign. Because there wasn't time as the motorcade was beginning to move, Michael told me he'd have it signed on the plane and send it back to me. Three days later, it arrived via FedEx. I opened it and there inside it read, *Dear Denise, Best Wishes, You Have a Great Husband, Donald Trump.* Understandably, she wasn't quite as thrilled as I was, but what an honor.

Weeks were flying by and we were having the time of our lives. Mr. Trump was shaking things up and the majority of people in New Hampshire loved him. Along with running the Keene campaign office, we were doing event after event. At this point, most times I was driving a staff car in the motorcade. On January 5, 2016, Mr. Trump was coming to a rally in Claremont, New Hampshire, and we were picking him and his staff up at the Lebanon airport. The runway there would not accommodate the Boeing 757, therefore Mr. Trump and some of his staff arrived in his Citation. I arrived at the airport two hours early as was protocol. There were three New Hampshire State Trooper vehicles and three Secret Service SUVs already there. We went through the bomb sweep process with the dog sniffing in and under every vehicle. Then we waited an hour or so for the Citation to arrive. While I didn't have much to do, the Secret Service agents were getting prepped. I was parked behind one of their SUVs when the back hatch lifted up. An agent got out with a long flat bag and laid it on the tailgate of the SUV. He proceeded to unzip it and pulled out an M-16 machine gun and went through a process of making sure it was ready to fire. He went in the vehicle, pulled out another, and performed the same task. He stood each gun straight up and positioned them in some type of stanchion on each side. Two other agents then got out and jumped up into the back of the SUV, sitting on a seat facing the rear. At any point of danger, they were ready and able to open the back window to fire if necessary. The back hatch closed down. It was then I began to realize this was becoming serious business. The other thought I had was, *I don't think I'm getting paid enough to do this job!*

Vermont, here we come. On January 7, 2016, we were scheduled for a rally in Burlington, Vermont, Bernie's backyard. No other Republican candidate made a visit the ultra-liberal state, and what a night Mr. Trump chose. Early January in upstate Vermont can be very cold, and this night was no exception. By nightfall, the temperature was in single digits and the wind chill was well below zero. Nevertheless, hearty Trump supporters began lining up by early afternoon and stood in the cold for hours to get into a 7:00 p.m. rally in a theater in downtown Burlington. It was amazing to see the interest and sacrifice people were willing to make to see Mr. Trump speak. Even Vermont had thousands of supporters, Republican and Democrats alike. Naturally, there were a few hundred wacko liberal loony tunes across the street from the theater with signs, yelling and screaming. The usual metal crowd control barriers and police were in front of them. They were like rabid animals, it was almost comical. So out of touch with reality and what America used to represent. I didn't drive this night as Mr. Trump flew into the Burlington Airport and I was doing crowd control at the rally.

My task was handling supporters coming through the front doors with another staff member and doing something we'd never done before. Because of the protesters who would sneak into our rallies and cause disruption, it was decided we would try and weed them out upon entry. Of course, it was later found out that Clinton's campaign was paying these people to start altercations so it would appear that Trump supporters were violent. These people have no moral character. As the crowd would pour in, we'd stop people and ask for their ticket. Then we'd ask, "Are you a Trump supporter?" There were several who responded "No," whereupon we'd step in front of them and inform them they were not invited in. Typical was the reaction of entitlement, some telling us they'd been in line for hours and therefore had a right to come in. I'll never forget one older woman, clearly a left wing loony, who, when I stopped her from walking forward by stepping in front of her, told me I couldn't throw her out. This was a public venue, she replied. I took much joy in informing her that this was an event paid for by Donald Trump and if she wasn't a supporter, she wasn't invited in. She continued to argue, at which point, I turned to the two police officers standing behind us and told them she wasn't allowed in. She flipped out, yelling at us and causing a scene. The officers took her by the arm, pulled her aside, and told her she could either leave immediately or would be arrested for trespassing. Someone later sent me a video clip from the nightly news of her telling a reporter of how she was manhandled and thrown out. Sweet justice, for once. Another memorable moment was the protester who made it inside by lying that he was a supporter, and then causing a raucous. A great memory was hearing Mr. Trump say to the police throwing him out, "Keep his coat, it's freezing out." Oh, the injustice! We loved it.

Another arrival into NH. Rain or shine,
Mr. Trump never missed an event

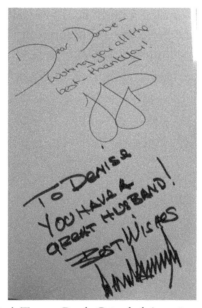

Denise's Trump Book Crippled America which
Ivanka and her father both signed

Don Trump Jr in our Keene NH Campaign Office

The Keene Campaign office mascot

Me speaking at Keene NH State College
on a debate night Fall 2015

Denise with Mr. Trump in NH

Picking up Mr. Trump arriving into Manchester NH Dec 2015

The Boss, Denise at the Keene NH Campaign Office

The Keene NH Campaign Office Denise and I ran

CHAPTER 6

Introduction to the Ground Campaign

Apparently, we weren't doing as well as we expected in the Iowa primary. Iowa and New Hampshire play a very important role in the presidential election process. They are the first two states in a series of nationwide party primary elections. Both states receive massive media coverage. The publicity and momentum can be enormous from a decisive win by a front-runner or better than expected result in the New Hampshire primary. It was determined that we didn't have much of a ground campaign in Iowa, the description being a door knocking campaign. After all, considering Mr. Trump was not a politician and no one was giving him a chance of winning, there were not a lot of experienced people running the show. I came to find out that no campaign can be successful without a strong door knocking campaign. Two weeks before the Vermont rally, Matt Ciepielowski called me and said, "We need someone to run the ground game and your name came up." I responded, "Great, I'm in. What's a ground game?"

Political Field Director Stuart Jolly had just arrived in New Hampshire to oversee our operation. Stuart was a retired U.S. Army colonel who turned out to be the absolute best leader I'd ever worked for. I'll always recall him telling me "I want you to own this, Sid. You can do this." Winning New Hampshire was paramount since it was the second state to vote in the primary. The upper staff knew I had a vast management background and was therefore a good choice to take on this important role. Never one to back away from a challenge, I had a crash course in how to run a presidential ground campaign. I learned quickly that what you needed were lots of volunteers. Mr. Trump had done so many rallies in New Hampshire to this point that we had thousands of names of people who wanted to help out. We had to quickly discern which ones were willing to go out walking all day in the cold, knocking on doors and asking questions. Fortunately, we had hundreds who were. This is when I began to have more of an appreciation for the sacrifice people were willing to make for the cause to make America great again.

Having the volunteers was only one piece of the puzzle. With each volunteer, I had to coordinate exactly when they could help out and what time duration they could allot in the field. Determine and keep track of how many people were arriving each day. Then make certain we had enough vehicles to transport volunteers to multiple cities and towns every day, seven days a week. People had to be broken into teams, and a team leader had to be determined for each one. So, quickly assessing someone with leadership skills became part of the job. Then there was coordinating where each team would go, to what town, and which neighborhoods without any crossover. I worked very closely with some of the support staff in New York at Trump Tower. Most importantly, Matt Braynard. Matt was the Director of Data and Strategy, and in particular, his talents were knowing where all the (R)epublicans, (D)emocrats, and (I)ndependents resided. Day and night, he was creating a database of selected areas in each town and city for our volunteers to knock doors. This information was delivered to me in numerical coordinates. These coordinates would then be uploaded to volunteers in the field via a cell phone app. Fortunately, I always kept up on the latest electronic gadgets and smart phones which made things a little easier.

Nevertheless, figuring out this app was a challenge in the field as every volunteer had to be trained as well. To make things more difficult, the app worked slightly different in an iPhone as it did in an Android system. Before we could begin sending out hundreds of people, I spent a week out knocking doors myself with a few of our die-hard volunteers. Two women in particular by the name of Daphne Papp and Paula Johnson. Paula and I were the first to take this app on a trial run in the city of Nashua. We'd walk from house to house until someone answered the door. After an introduction, there were several questions in the app which required answers, such as which were the most important current national issues to that person, ending with who they were planning on voting for in the primary. If they were on the fence, we'd do our best to persuade them to see why Mr. Trump should be their choice. We did this for a week, and then I began to organize other volunteers. Daphne would drive all the way from Gloucester, Massachusetts, to help out every day. She was funny, vibrant, and dedicated, along with being a tireless worker. We really hit it off and I could count on her every day to give one hundred percent. We had a lot fun and we became close friends to this day.

I came to learn that a campaign office is a very strange place. There are people of every walk of life coming and going, day and night. Some came in to do phone banking, some to knock doors, some to get signs for their yard or for their friends and family, some came in to bloviate about how great they were for many reasons, and there was always the campaign office screwball—the one who would drive everyone nuts. They likely had few friends and there was always plenty of free food, plus someone to talk to. The things people would do and say would sometimes leave us bewildered. Then there were the *yahoos*. The volunteers who had huge egos told everyone how much they did but you never saw them roll up their sleeves, phone bank for hours, or go out in the cold, knocking on doors. State reps and leadership who bloviated at rallies about how much they did, having their picture taken with Mr. Trump over and over. We often talked about how nice it would've been if they'd give their time in the spotlight to someone who was actually working, volunteering their time and money to come to New Hampshire to help. It was somewhat sad and pathetic.

By the middle of January, we had two busloads of New Yorkers come to New Hampshire to help us out. I needed to arrange accommodations, how we'd feed them morning, noon, and night, and coordinate the logistics of how we pick them up from their hotels and get them into teams. Some did phone banking which was the easy part. We arranged to have the bottom floor of a large office building in downtown Manchester be the workspace for meeting and phone banking. I rented five twelve-passenger vans for a week. Their charter buses would bring them to the office building in the morning, and I'd have a team leader for each van waiting to be loaded. We'd do app training, load up each van, and out we'd go for the day, snow or rain. I have to hand it to those New Yorkers, they were a hardy bunch. We had a couple of significant snowstorms that week but nothing kept us grounded, and they were up for the challenge from Mother Nature. These teams and team leaders gritted it out in the cold and heavy snow from morning until dusk and never complained. I had to keep a steady supply of hand and feet warmers, along with cell phone battery chargers available every day. At this point, while my teams were out, I planned with Matt Braynard on where we needed to focus our efforts the next day, ran for supplies, helped to train phone bankers, and occasionally went out knocking with a team. Each night around nine or ten o'clock, I'd take each van to gas it up for the next day. My life was like a tornado in the Manchester headquarters by 7:00 a.m. and leave around 10:30 p.m., seven days a week. All of the staff did this as we were deeply committed. We had a state to win for Mr. Trump.

During this time, there were three men in particular who I came to depend on as door knocking team leaders; men who we would later deem *super volunteers*. My friend Jason Squeglia from northern Massachusetts, Charles Bruckerhoff from Connecticut and Robert Bowes from Maryland. These three men were the most dedicated individuals I'd ever met. They were working with us at least seventy hours a week for free. Charles was paying for his own hotel accommodations for weeks. These guys made an enormous impact on us winning New Hampshire in the primary. I'll never forget the day Jason, Charles, Daphne, and I were out knocking on doors. We were all getting accustomed to the phone app. We pulled up in front of a house in Manchester. It was decided Daphne and Charles would go up and knock. As they were waiting for someone to come to the door, the window beside the front stairs opened. There, leaning out was a scantily clad young woman in bra and thong. Her friend, dressed similarly, leaned out the window with her. Daphne and Charles did their best to ask some questions, apparently with Charles stuttering profusely. They came back to the SUV laughing hysterically, with Charles being beet red. We got a lot of mileage from that one.

Denise ran the Keene Campaign office for the last month and a half and did an incredible job, along with our stellar intern from Keene State College, Nicole Gleason. She supplied the whole western part of the state with signs and support, holding meetings, and just making it happen. For the last month and a half leading up to the primary, we only saw each other late at night for a short time. Little did we know it was a sacrifice that paled compared to what was ahead. But we always made time to pray and thank the Lord for using us in this capacity. The bond we'd developed through this was now unbreakable. We worked so hard together month after month, always supporting each other's struggles each day. We were blessed and so very grateful! People by the thousands volunteered all over the state in so many capacities. Make America Great Again was the Trump mantra and everyone bought into it, everyone except the New Hampshire GOP and Republican Senator Kelly Ayotte.

Ayotte refused to support Mr. Trump, and the GOP was led by Jennifer Horn, not a very well-liked woman in many corners of the state. She managed to raise the ire of many of the Republican State party leaders with her snooty, brash attitude. In a November 25, 2015, article in the Boston Globe Horn said this, "Shallow campaigns that depend on bombast and divisive rhetoric do not succeed in New Hampshire, and I don't expect that they will now." We never doubted that Mr. Trump wasn't going to win the state, and despite Horn and the GOP, we did. By February ninth, we had knocked on tens of thousands of doors, made the impact we needed to, and won New Hampshire. Mr. Trump had done his part, and so did we. There was a huge celebration at a venue in Manchester. It accommodated only a few hundred people and there must've been a thousand in line, all standing out in the freezing cold to celebrate this historic event. Denise and I got to enter through a side door since we were staff members and were right up front for the celebration. The entire Trump family came out on stage to blaring music, along with Corey,

Michael, and Stuart. We celebrated for a couple of hours, and then left. It was awesome. Mr. Trump thanked everyone for the win, Little did I know the best was yet to come.

Celebrating with staff and volunteers in NH. Many of these folks would come on staff and joined us later in other states

Arrival into Portsmoth NH on a snowy Saturday.
Secret Service, State Troopers and staff cars parked
inside a hanger while we await de-icing

De-icing the big 757 before departure from
Portsmouth Pease Air Force Base

Denise and I with NH Deputy State Director Andrew Georgevits.
Andrew was the catalyst through the entire NH Primary

Denise and I with our leader, Field Director Stuart
Jolly after we got our first win, New Hampshire

Lowell Ma Trump rally with BIG Fred Smerlas. Ex-Buffalo
Bill and New England Patriot, great guy. Man was he huge

Mr. Trump and his family as we celebrated the
New Hampshire win Feb 9th 2016

Mr. Trump visiting the Manchester NH
campaign office late 2015

National Field Director Stuart Jolly and I
after our win in the NH primary

Pic taken out the right side window of my staff car as
we began our circle to the other side for pickup

Portsmouth NH Jan 2016. Any other
candidate would've canceled the event

Mr. Trump and I at the Manchester NH HQ early 2016

Three Secret Service vehicles in front of my staff car
for pick up at Lebanon NH airport Jan 2016

CHAPTER 7

No Time to Waste—on to South Carolina

S hortly before Election Day, Campaign Manager Corey Lewondowski, Political Director Michael Glassner, and Field Director Stuart Jolly had decided that if we pulled off New Hampshire, it would springboard the campaign to a win in South Carolina next. They had decided they had such a strong team of staffers in New Hampshire, why not send some of us forward to do what we had done so well? State Director Matt Ciepielowski and Stuart Jolly approached me on February 8. The question, "Are you willing to go forward and run the ground campaign in the most important states to come along in the primary?" I was honored to be asked but I wanted to discuss it with Denise, although I knew what her answer would be. She was behind the idea 100 percent. Her response was that we had come this far, there was no stopping now. The Lord had put us here for a reason, and we knew what we had to do.

By this point, Denise and I firmly believed that there was divine intervention happening around the Trump campaign quest. God was gradually being eliminated from society in America, and the PC culture was like a parasitic plant that chokes the life out of other plants. We felt in our hearts that God was looking down on America and frowning, but He had decided enough was enough. We knew it would be difficult as I would be gone for up to six weeks at a time. We enjoyed our win together on February 9 and prepared to say goodbye two days later. I began packing the next day and was on a plane to South Carolina on February 11. When we arrived at the airport, we picked up a handful of rental cars already reserved for us. We would use these for our door knocking teams. One of the best things we enjoyed about being in South Carolina—it was warm! At last, we were out of the cold. We loved it. The Greenville headquarters was perfect; one of the nicest we'd seen. Deputy State Director James Epley greeted us on the morning of February 12. We discussed strategies, the volunteer base, and where we needed to focus our efforts door knocking in the state. This information was all relayed back to New York, and strategic counties, cities, and towns were determined quickly. I then needed to get this information to the other campaign offices along with the app information, app training videos, and instructions of where to send people, along with daily and weekly goals.

When we arrived in a state, the leadership handed Matt and I the keys to the office, literally. They were instructed to accommodate us in every way possible, and we had control from there to their primary date. The leadership in South Carolina could not have been more accommodating. Mr. Trump came to South Carolina shortly after we arrived. This was always the impetus to getting volunteers coming in to help. We had busloads of people come down from North Carolina to help us as well. Some people phone banked, and others went out door knocking. As we found in New Hampshire, people of all sorts came in to volunteer. The support for Mr. Trump was incredible. One real novelty, which Deputy State Director James Eply had arranged, was two medium sized RVs. But not just plain RVs, these had Mr. Trump's pictures and logo, *Make America Great Again,* all over them. They were special and really drew attention. We could fit about nine volunteers in each one and ran them from morning to night, neighborhood after neighborhood. I arranged a driver and copilot in each so we didn't lose track of where we left people off.

Our teams would hit a neighborhood, drop two people on one street with coordinates of houses to knock on, then continue on dropping two more a few streets away and so on. We'd come back around, pick up, and move on to another designated area. In many neighborhoods, people would come out of their houses, thinking Mr. Trump was in the RV. We would give them yard signs and bumper stickers. They loved it and so did our volunteers. We would pull the RVs off the road when Mr. Trump came to South Carolina for a rally. We would park them outside the rally, load them with yard signs, and distribute thousands of signs to people. What a hit these RVs were, and what a hit Mr. Trump was in South Carolina. Same as New Hampshire, we worked eighty-five to ninety hours every single week. I would typically open the campaign office by about seven o'clock in the morning as I had to finish prepping to get teams ready to go by eight-thirty. One constant was fast food. We had to feed the volunteer's lunch and dinners every day. We purchased hundreds of dollars of burgers, pizza, Chinese food, and fried chicken every day of the week. There was no time for us to go out to eat, so we all ate fast food on the run every day.

Getting all the volunteers organized and trained, along with making sure the RVs had plenty of handout materials and were loaded with plenty of bottled water, was my most stressful parts of every day. No sooner would you have most of the volunteers ready when one person would need to get something or have some small issue. The next thing you know, the rest of the team is wandering around talking. Then, it was pulling the whole team back together and pushing them out the door. It was like herding puppies! Fortunately for me, three of my very best team leaders—Jason, Charles and Robert came down to South Carolina to continue working with us. These guys helped me keep my sanity. I leaned on them a lot, and again, could not have done my job without them. Mr. Trump came into the Greenville office while we were there and thanked everyone for their help, volunteers and all. We even had infamous Trump supporters, Diamond and Silk, come into the Greenville office. They were terrific and a lot of fun to be around. A comical memory was, one day I gave my rental car keys to one of our New Hampshire staffers, Josh Whitehouse. Josh had the best last name of anyone. He was using my car to lead a door knocking team. When he was done at the end of the day, he parked the car back in the parking garage. When I went to leave, I could not find the car so I naturally pressed the remote alarm button. Did you ever try denoting where an alarm sound is coming from in an eight-story parking garage? All you'd hear was an echo. I went up and down, one side to the other trying to locate that car. After an hour, I found it parked on the first floor. Lesson learned!

It also was here in Greenville where I had my first contact with who would become my archnemesis, Nancy Mace. Nancy was running the Columbia, South Carolina, campaign office and did not take instruction well. My first interaction with her was on the phone, letting her know exactly where we needed to focus our efforts and how I wanted her to go about accomplishing our goal in the Columbia area. She immediately pushed back, telling me that is not how she had been doing things. I politely informed her that Stuart Jolly had given me the mandate of running the ground campaign in the state and she needed to do what I was asking her. We had a common goal and it was going to be done the way I had asked her. She hung up and placed a call to Stuart. Being the professional leader he was, Stuart told her that I was in charge and she was to follow the instructions I had given her. Stuart's long career in the army was all about following the chain of command. I learned not long after this that Nancy was the first woman to graduate from The Citadel, one of six senior military colleges. Apparently, at one time, this was a male only college and Nancy had sued the college to get in. The rule of thumb is, graduating cadets join the Army. Not Nancy. She dissed the Army upon graduation. She was a woman who was used to getting her way, and she did not like me one bit.

We were informed on February 18 that we would be departing for Texas on primary day, the twentieth of February. Nancy was difficult to work with, but she had other strengths which I recognized might be helpful in Texas. I went to Stuart Jolly and requested that we bring her with us if she was willing. He agreed, although this was a decision I would firmly regret. All of the campaign offices in South Carolina were outfitted with dozens of folding chairs, office chairs, printers, office supplies, signs of variable sizes, and mini refrigerators. As the primary ended, each office was closed. There was no need to pay for rent until we went to the general election if we won. It was decided that we would pack up each campaign office, rent a large

U-Haul, put the contents of each office in it, and drive it to Texas. I had suggested that we bring the RVs to Texas as well, and Corey and Michael agreed. We constantly had to fight off the media. They would show up and walk into the campaign office with cameras rolling. It was no secret by this time there was no love lost on the liberal media from Mr. Trump. All except for Fox News, the rest were doing everything they could to hurt our campaign. We would back them right out the door, not welcome! February 20, primary day rolled around and we accomplished another goal—we won South Carolina. The left wing media was having palpitations. The unimaginable was happening, Mr. Trump and his band of misfits were accomplishing what they said was impossible.

Greenville SC campaign office. The best one we had

I was sitting across from Stuart Jolly and infamous
Trump supporters Diamond and Silk

Mr. Trump coming into the Greenville SC office
to thank staff and volunteers for our help

Our two Trump RV's would pull people out
of their houses everywhere we went

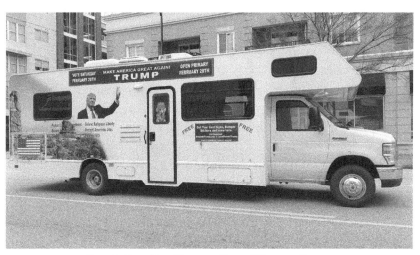

South Carolina Deputy State Director James
Epley was the first to get us these

CHAPTER 8

Ted Cruz, Here We Come

B efore we left for Texas, the plan was made to split up our team which was now growing. New Hampshire State Director Matt Ciepielowski headed up our strike team and was a great leader, incredibly mature for twenty-six years old. Matt and I sat and discussed whom to send where. We had campaign offices in Dallas, San Antonio, Houston, and Austin. After this decision was made, everyone's name and information had to be emailed to our travel department headed up by a young gentleman by the name of John McEntee. John came to Greenville and began showing up in states where Mr. Trump was arriving. He was a very sharp, always well-dressed young executive. I would gradually work closer with John as I took on the responsibility of deciding what hotels we were going to stay in. Along with that, I would decide what vehicles we would need to pick up at the airport. It was obvious that we could get more feet on the street with larger SUVs rather than cars. In addition, we needed to carry water, signs, and handout material with each team as well. Nancy Mace, Zach Montanaro, a New Hampshire staffer, and I landed in Dallas late afternoon of February 20 and headed for the LaQuinta Inn. When John McEntee and his staff made our reservations, there was no way to know precisely what part of town the hotel was located.

A pattern was developing with state staff where we were headed to next. Typically in place long before we'd arrive, they'd choose a campaign office based on how cheap the rent was. In some cases, Dallas being one of them, the office selected was in a very seedy part of the city. Along with that came a very seedy hotel with torn, stained furniture, broken toilet seats, and stained carpets. It was here that I began taking control of where we were going to stay in upcoming travels. Hello, Marriot Suites? I moved about five miles away and there I stayed. Nancy, Zach, and a couple of other volunteers who drove the RVs and U-Haul didn't have as nasty of a room as I did, and they decided they'd stay. The next morning, we met the Texas Deputy State Director Eric Marhoum at the Dallas campaign office. I got out of my car and my jaw dropped. Over the front door, mounted twenty feet up on the front of the building was *Wine and Beer*. We met and walked inside and discovered three out of four walls were empty cooler chests, as you would expect in a beer store. I could not believe what I was seeing and took Eric outside. I pointed to the sign and asked him if he thought that might be a problem considering Mr. Trump doesn't drink alcohol of any kind. If left in place, the media would have a field day.

The property owner said he would see what he could do to get the sign taken down. The next challenge, how do we hide cooler doors from the media who would inevitably be circling like vultures? Off to Walmart we went to find rolls of paper to cover them. As the day went on, we began scraping the beer signs off the top of the walls and cleaning. The electricity had not been turned on yet and there was no internet for the phone system. Considering we only had ten days to make an impact, things were not looking up. I was beyond frustrated and had to make a decision. Was this office going to be up and running in time to be operational or not? One of the volunteers helping us clean mentioned to me that she had told the Texas staff that she could've helped with a much-preferred office on the other side of Dallas but was ignored. I asked other questions and soon had the name and number of a Texas businessman named Ron Broadway. One of Ron's business partners was an office developer who had available space in an office complex on the first floor, perfectly suited.

I called Matt Ciepielowski, who was running the Austin office, and described our dilemma. Matt agreed, and we moved ASAP. I jumped in my rental and began the not so short journey across Dallas to meet Brian Brown, Ron's friend. The office was enormous, carpeted, clean, and ready. Brian could have internet ready within a day, and he and Ron would take care of the rent. Matt decided to head to Dallas because of the situation. There was one problem. Hero-at-large and New Hampshire staffer Jonathan Dimock had gotten wind that we needed to move out of the Dallas office. Some people in life want to be helpful just because it's the right thing to do. Then there are some who have a motive of making themselves look good. Dimock fits the later. I received a call from Matt—*Cip*, as we called him—shortly after meeting up with Brian Brown. Apparently, Dimock found a rental office as well and Matt wanted us to see that one, too, as it wasn't as far away as the other. I got the address and drove there to meet this person at about 9:00 p.m. Jonathan and a couple of others showed up at the same time. As I'm about to introduce myself, Jonathan steps forward, business card in hand, stating he's the IT manager.

I stepped aside as we toured the building. It was run down but certainly would've worked. The main questions as always, how soon can we get electricity and internet? The building owner's answer was "The next day." He had to go to City Hall and pay the electric bill. Something didn't smell right about this guy. It was determined to get prepared to move into this building without a signed a lease. I strongly suggested this was not a good idea as we were not allowed by our legal department to take possession of an office before the lease is signed. In addition, we had no firm answer as to when we would have power and internet. Dimock pushed the move, confident *his* guy would come through. The U-Haul from South Carolina needed to drop half the truck and keep going to one of the other offices. So Dimock and a few volunteers stayed at this building that night and unloaded dozens of chairs, tables, thousands of yard signs, along with office supplies.

As we rolled into the next day, it apparently became clear to Matt Cip and Stuart Jolly that this landlord was not going to come through. We received instructions to move into Brian Brown's office space. I had a contract sent to him immediately. By the end of the day, Brian confirmed internet would be installed the next morning and there was already power supplied. I had to go rent a U-Haul, and that night, a bunch of us spent about two hours packing up everything that was dropped the night before. I was not a happy camper. I had rented a midsize U-Haul and this thing was packed to the brim. I was typically the oldest person on staff and when the question arose who was going to drive the U-Haul, no one volunteered. They were all afraid to because of how packed and heavy it was. As it turned out, I didn't blame them as I needed to start braking about two hundred feet sooner than typical to stop the damn thing. We dropped the truck at the new office at about 1:00 a.m. and would unload it the next morning. Fortunately we only had to drive around the corner to arrive at our new hotel, and were up at 6:00 a.m., then off to get the new office up and running.

Matt Cip was working to blast out emails from our software program where people had sent in information that they wanted to volunteer and there were thousands of them. Before long, we had people of all sorts walking through the door. Phone systems were up and the internet was working. We began differentiating between phone bankers and door knockers. All of this had taken so much time away from more important tasks, such as prepping for where we needed to focus our efforts in the field. I began sending coordinates and instructions to the other offices of where to focus their efforts. My friends Jason and Charles were sent to other cities as they were becoming an integral part of the ground campaign. They both were great leaders, as well as devoted to the cause of Making America Great Again. I missed them dearly, but we made do and found others willing to take that role, albeit less effectively. At this point, I was missing Denise a lot. I hadn't been to church in weeks and was missing that connection with God to which I had begun leaning on for strength.

I had never actually driven in and around Texas before, and had only flown in and out of Dallas over the years. We constantly went past churches which were ten times the size I'd ever seen before.

Having been raised in Massachusetts, the churches in the Northeast pale to the size of churches in Texas. Someone had told me that it was not uncommon to have a following of ten thousand people for some churches. I thought what a great place to park our RVs and hand out yard signs and bumper stickers. So I called the First Baptist Church of Dallas and inquired into the possibility. I spoke with a pastor who explained that although Senior Pastor Robert Jeffress was a Trump supporter and most of the congregation were as well, it wasn't something they could agree to. My interpretation, the PC culture was still too strong. However, it did not keep me from going there for the service the following Sunday.

I asked Stuart Jolly if he'd care to join me. He and I attended a service in the most remarkable church I had ever seen. Stuart is from the South and has a deep commitment to his faith in God—another reason I admired him. We drove into downtown Dallas, parked, and went into this enormous beautiful building. Walking into this church is breathtaking—seating for thousands of people, an enormous stage, full orchestra, and about fifty choir singers behind the stage. The music, along with four singers, gave me goosebumps. Pastor Jeffress came out and gave an inspiring message. At the end, Stuart had to take a call from Michael Glassner, so I went down to the front by myself to meet Pastor Jeffress and introduce myself. I was wearing a suit, and as always, had my Trump staff pin on my lapel. When I told him I was the ground campaign manager for Mr. Trump, he beamed. He then put his hand on my shoulder and said a prayer for Mr. Trump, myself, and all of us in the campaign, thanking me for my service. This campaign was more humbling than anything that I had ever experienced. I realized even more how very fortunate I was to be given this opportunity. I couldn't wait to tell Denise. Praise the Lord.

Mr. Trump was doing a daytime rally in Fort Worth one day and we decided to load up both of the Trump RVs with thousands of yard signs and headed down. One of the more humorous moments happened before the crowd came out. Deputy State Director Eric Marhoum introduced me to his mother, a very well-dressed woman in her fifties in a short skirt and black boots with spiked heels. She was Mexican and a true Trumper, somewhat boisterous and a little zany but a sweetheart. When Eric told her my position in the campaign, she was all over me. At some point, I was able to move away from her and happened to run into Stuart Jolly who had come outside as the event was almost over. I put my arm around Stuart and proclaimed, "I have someone very important for you to meet." He knew by my smile that he might not like this and warned me. I took him over to Eric's mother and introduced him as the big cheese—the big guy! She was on him like a bear on honey, hugging and kissing him. Of course, I could not stop laughing as Stuart mouthed, "I'm gonna kill you."

The rally ended and supporters, sometimes twenty deep, swarmed us. It was awesome seeing the support for Mr. Trump in Texas. Of course, being this close to Mexico, there were demonstrators yelling about Trump's stance on immigration—illegal immigration that is. I still do not understand how people felt Mr. Trump's stance was so wrong. Every other country in the world keeps their borders closed, including Mexico! However, we are supposed to simply let immigrants pour through our borders untouched and absorb the expense. In 2014, over 300,000 pregnant illegal immigrants came into this country to have their babies in U.S. hospitals. All at US taxpayers' expense, and for the simple reason they and their baby would then become U.S. citizens. The majorities then go on welfare and further feed off our system. I'm sorry, but this is taking advantage of our laws. This was one of the main reasons Denise and I supported Mr. Trump. A country without borders is not a safe country, not in today's world. Not to mention the drug trade coming from South America and through Mexico.

As we drove the RVs back to Dallas, it was interesting to watch the reaction from people on the highway. All stared, some honked their horns and gave us thumbs up, and then some would give us the finger. Whereas, we would simply smile, wave, and laugh, knowing our existence pissed them off. We got back late afternoon and it was back to the real work. That night, I remember going into the printer/snack room in the office and there was a very large American flag thrown in a pile on top of the printer. I was steaming and went right to whom I had last seen with that flag—twenty-three-year old New

Hampshire staffer Zack Montanaro. I asked him if he had thrown the flag in there on the printer. His response was "Yes." My next statement, "Go pick it up and fold it!" Some might say "Big deal." Moreover, I say that is part of what's wrong with this country—lack of respect. Perhaps if Zack had fought for his country, as so many have, he would have more appreciation for what our flag stands for. Zack's laid-back, *I don't really care attitude* wore on me, and by the end of two more states, he was left home in New Hampshire. We did not have room for deadweight, and if you were not there to give one hundred percent, then stay home. This was way too important!

A couple of days before the March first Texas primary vote, we were told by Stuart that next up was Ohio. Because of what happened with the hotel in Dallas, I made it a point to find out which cities would be our destination ahead of time. Matt and I decided which personnel were going where, and I began locating which hotels to book. After all, it wasn't as though we were only staying there for a night or two. At this point, John McEntee had entrusted me with his Trump for President American Express card, and travel agent gradually became part of my job. It was this or chance staying in another squalor hotel. As it turned out, Ted Cruz kicked our asses but it wasn't from lack of effort, that's for sure. I don't believe we were sent there thinking we would win. I believe it was just to stick it in Cruz's face since we were the front-runner in the overall poles. We all got to fly home for a day and a half, and then it was off to Ohio. The RVs were sent to Florida to be used to take down *low energy* Jeb. Mr. Trump was positioning himself well, and Corey, Michael, and Stuart had us pointed in the right direction. Running the ground campaign was giving me a pretty good feel for what was happening, and I never doubted we would not win this thing.

Dallas Campaign Office full of volunteers watching a debate

Fort Worth Texas Trump rally. One of
the few times I attended these

Inside the First Baptist Church of Dallas

This volunteer saved our bacon in Dallas. She hooked
me up with Ron Broadway to get this office

We added Mr. Trumps cutout to the mix of greats in Dallas

CHAPTER 9

The Heartland of America

We had less than two weeks to make an impact in Ohio. There were prearranged offices in Lorain, Middleburg Heights, and Columbus. Matt was running Columbus, Nancy Mace was running Middleburg Heights, and I had Lorain, lucky me. I was quickly finding out how the Lord tests us and challenges our strength. The Lorain office was virtually in a ghetto, located in a small strip mall, and sat in front of a homeless shelter. The poverty rate in Lorain is one of the highest in the state, and I assure you there were not many Trump supporters nearby. There was no heat in the office, and in early March, just a couple of blocks from Lake Erie is not exactly warm. Nonetheless, we began setting up the office and blasting out emails of our location in order to get volunteers. Strange thing was, nobody was showing up, except the homeless guys begging for food. One lady pulled up in front, came in for a couple of signs, and told us there was no way she was door knocking around here, then left. I thought to myself, *Oh no, not again!* We had to make this office work; we didn't have time to move again. Our crew began putting yard signs together anyway, and we pushed on. The next day, we got more deliveries of signs and piled boxes into the back of the office. At one point, a group of young black men walked by, stopping to pound on the glass and yelling profanities about Mr. Trump. I called the police who then began to keep a closer eye on us. It became clear to me, there was no way we were going to get volunteers into this office in sufficient quantity to make any impact and we had to move. Lord help us!

Every minute we lost being productive was crucial. We just couldn't afford losing hours of phone banking and door knocking time, but we were about to. We were again in a state with a strong presidential candidate running against us—Governor John Kasich. Ohio loved him, for the most part. Kasich opened the door in Ohio to fracking in 2011 which is hydraulic fracturing with horizontal drilling into the earth to locate natural gas and oil. It created many jobs and was supposed to be a boom for families but it never transpired that way. Kasich was part of the establishment to thousands of Ohioans and they wanted Trump, but it was an uphill battle just like Texas. I worked out a deal with the hotel we were staying at to rent their conference room. We got tablets and headsets all set up and we were ready to rock. This became our campaign office and we blasted out emails to supporters of our new location. Before long, we had people coming in to phone bank and door knock. Fortunately, this time I had Jason Squeglia with us, and Jason stepped up as always and took a leadership role in making it happen. He was a relentless leader in door knocking and a great example. There was no loafing for people on his team. We had the greatest admiration for each other and were becoming good friends.

My other trusted soldier and friend, Charles Bruckerhoff, was working in the Middleburg Heights office with Nancy Mace. When we were closing in on primary day, I'll never forget Charles calling me and telling me this: "If I have to be under the management of Nancy Mace going forward, I'd rather go home." I also had a volunteer from South Carolina who helped us in Dallas and came to Ohio to help out. She was also working in the Middleburg Heights office. She called me one day to tell me she was going to another part of the state where her parents lived and would knock doors on her own. She said she wasn't going to be treated like a sixteen-year-old by Nancy any longer and off she went. Apparently, Nancy had a very demeaning and demoralizing management style that just wasn't working well, and nobody wanted to address it yet.

There was always something which needed to be addressed nearly every day in each state to this point—either some nutty volunteer or staff issue that I had to address. Ohio wasn't any different. We had brought a young Army veteran from Texas with us to Ohio—Thomas. He was a great phone banker in the Dallas office and would show up nearly every day. He always dressed nicely, and would go around emptying trash and helping in whatever way he could. He addressed everyone as Sir or Ma'am, but there was something a little odd about him. I came to find out his vehicle had been blown up by an IED in Iraq and messed up his head just a bit. While in Texas, he had asked me, if he paid his own way, could we utilize him in Ohio? I told him yes, and he drove to Lorain, Ohio, with another volunteer. I soon regretted this decision as well. There was a restaurant directly across from the hotel, which also had a bar, and most of the guys would go over at night for a few beers.

On this particular night, apparently, Thomas had one too many. I later learned that he was on medication which didn't mix well with alcohol. The next day, I was told that he got into a nasty argument with a female bartender and started calling her some very vulgar words. Some of the guys had to pull him out before it got worse. That's all we needed to be a headline in the newspaper: "Trump staff and volunteers involved in bar fight." So the next night, I called a meeting of staff, our *super volunteers*, and Thomas. I reviewed what I was told happened at the bar and pointed out how drinking in a bar is a recipe for problems and bad publicity. I then turned to Thomas and directed my frustration with him for calling a bartender foul names. He blew up, yelling that he was the scapegoat and "You're not pissed off at the other guys." This was going from bad to worse, so I calmed the situation down and addressed everyone in terms of not letting this happen again. The next morning, Thomas didn't show up in the conference room to do phone banking. By early afternoon, no one had seen him.

Now knowing that his cheese was sliding off his cracker, I feared the worst and headed for his hotel room. I knocked on his door for a few minutes with no answer. I was praying he wasn't inside hanging from the shower rod or worse. I went down to the front desk and inquired if anyone had seen him when I was told he had checked out a few hours ago. He had quietly left and flew home to Texas without saying a word. I figured that was the end of that problem until I received a call from Stuart Jolly about a week later asking me what happened with this guy Thomas. Apparently, he'd flown to New York City and tried to get into Trump Tower in order to see Mr. Trump and tell him how I abused a veteran. He threatened to go to CNN and Fox News if I wasn't terminated. That wasn't going to happen and we were sure the networks must have seen what a screwball he was, so nothing ever transpired. I thought, *Too bad I hadn't seen this coming a few weeks earlier.*

Although we knocked on tens of thousands of doors and persuaded a lot of people to vote for Trump, we lost Ohio. Kasich won all the delegates, but we still picked up nearly three quarters of a million votes if we made it to the general election. This state made more of an impact on me than any, thus far, in terms of how it reflected what was happening in our country. Nearly everywhere we went, we saw storefronts boarded up and abandoned factories, rundown neighborhoods and a low quality of life. I will never forget a fifty-something gentleman who came in to volunteer. He said to me, "I've been a Democrat my whole life but I'm voting for Trump. I worked at a steel mill for almost thirty years and was laid off because the company moved to Mexico. I work a part-time retail job now and try to do some contracting, and even that's difficult. For example, I went to a local Hotel 6 being built to try and get some work. There were so many illegal immigrants working on the job for half of what I can afford to work for, they wouldn't hire me." I was heartbroken for this man and I knew there were hundreds of thousands more just like him. He represented one of the main issues of what Mr. Trump was telling everyone, and we had a close-up view.

It's truly fascinating how God puts people in our lives when needed the most. It had again been a little while since I had been able to get to church. One day, after our teams had all dispersed for the day, a gentleman came in to help phone bank. He was warm, friendly, and articulate. I couldn't help but notice the cross hanging around his neck. We began talking about the state of the country, and he mentioned God in the conversation. His name was Hap Halter. Before I knew it, we were sharing stories about our faith. Hap was fascinated as to how I came to be saved by the Lord. I came to find out, Hap was a pastor at the nearby Faith Lutheran Church in Avon, Ohio, and invited me to his service that upcoming Sunday. I gladly accepted and took my friend Andrew Coffield with me. Andrew was a great kid, a fellow Trump staffer from Ohio, and a fellow Christian. It was rejuvenating to walk into God's dwelling again. Clearly, the Lord was making sure to keep my faith strong, and I was very grateful for Him putting Hap Halter in my life.

A few days before the end of the Ohio primary, Matt Ciepielowski came up from the Columbus office to our hotel/campaign office. He asked me if I would be willing to forego an upcoming short trip home. Our next stop was Wisconsin and there were no prearranged campaign offices there. We were going to fly out a couple of days before the rest of the team and solidify offices in strategic areas. This would mean being gone from home for a month and a half, so I called Denise and filled her in on what I needed to do. We believed the Lord was guiding us to do what was necessary so the decision was easy, but I missed my life at home. I began to have more of an appreciation of how difficult it must be for our military personnel who are gone from home for several months at a time. The next day, Matt, Josh Whitehouse, and I boarded a plane for Milwaukee.

Jason and some of our team inside the Lorain Ohio office

Our Lorain Ohio campaign office. What a nightmare

DO'S AND DON'TS OF DOOR KNOCKING

DO'S

- Get your team leaders cell number
- Know the script well
- Know Mr. Trumps policy issues so you can talk about them
- Engage undecided people/ask them what issue is important to them
- If they say "Yes" ask them if they'd like a lawn sign
- Sync your app while you're walking
- Come back again to help and bring a friend

DON'TS

- Never argue with anyone no matter what
- Walk away from rude people/don't engage
- Don't allow someone to keep you talking too long
- Don't forget to sync before you logout at the end of your day
- Don't speak for the campaign/discuss your own personal viewpoints

Yes I had to make things very clear

CHAPTER 10

Wisconsin and a Trip to the ER

We landed in Wisconsin the morning of March 13. It had been decided we'd open an office around Milwaukee, and another close to Green Bay. There wasn't a minute to waste as we hadn't made hotel or rental vehicle reservations for the rest of the team yet which now totaled fifteen. Sitting in the airport, Josh and I began searching on our laptops for real estate rentals on every site we could find. Matt was handling other issues with Corey and Stuart. Most property owners did not want to rent their office space for only three weeks, so it took a lot of phone calls. I ended up finding us an office in Menomonee Falls just outside of Milwaukee, and another in Appleton just outside of Green Bay. Fortunately, both location owners were Trump supporters. We had to see each one first, and I had arranged a time to meet at each one. We grabbed our luggage and headed for our SUV. The office in Menomonee Falls was sublevel with a spiral staircase going down from the ground floor. It also had an elevator which we could use for bringing down thousands of signs which would be delivered in a few days. The setup wasn't perfect but it would do, so I got moving to get a lease sent to New York and we were off to Appleton next.

The Appleton office was perfect in terms of layout and the owner was very accommodating. Both locations would have internet the next day and we'd be ready to rock and roll. I began the exercise of locating hotels and arranging rental vehicles. Matt had already made arrangements for half of our team to land in Milwaukee and half into Green Bay. We decided to put Nancy Mace in Appleton and provide her with all the younger staff members and volunteers who were now part of our Strike Team. Perhaps that would help keep the peace in her office and there would be less dissention, although as the weeks went on, there were still grumblings of unhappiness among the troops working under her tutelage. While I worked on precisely where we were focusing on our door knocking campaign, Matt, Josh, and Dimock were setting up email blasts to Wisconsin Trump supporters.

My Texas friend Ron Broadway called shortly before we arrived in Wisconsin, and again helped us out with rent for the offices. It wasn't that Mr. Trump needed the help, it was more that Ron and his friends wanted to help the cause—all great Americans. We arranged an open house for both offices via emails to Republicans around Milwaukee and Green Bay. Both offices were deluged with volunteers. We had a line of people going out the door, up the spiral staircase, and outside. It was inspiring to see the support for Mr. Trump. We took names and numbers, provided food and refreshments, and began organizing our effort in the state. In short order, we were sending out hundreds of door knocking teams all around Milwaukee and Green Bay. Dozens of people phone banking, seven days a week in both offices. In every state, we fed the volunteers' lunch and dinner every day—fast food and more fast food. We were getting to the point where we never wanted to see pizza again, ever! So we mixed it up with burgers and fries, Chinese food, and fried chicken.

One day, I started to get a stomachache—a rarity for me. Two days later, I still had it. Five days later, I knew something was wrong as it never went away. The Saturday afternoon before Easter, I gave in and went to the local emergency room in Menomonee Falls. They did a bunch of tests and found I had a bleeding ulcer. Eighty-five to ninety hours every week and months of fast food was taking its toll on me. They gave me medicine intravenously which took the pain away, finally. The doctor suggested I stay for a scope on Sunday, but there was no assurance that a doctor would be there on Easter

Sunday and I'd be there until Monday. My pain was gone and I fig-ured I'd take my chances with the prescription they gave me. Four hours later, I was on my way back to the campaign office and back to doing my job. I'd be damned if a bleeding ulcer was going to keep me down, we had a state to win and nobody else on the team knew the ground game like I did. I couldn't burden my teammates. Denise and I prayed, and the Lord blessed us again. Going forward, I forced myself to go out and get better food at lunch and dinner which helped my situation.

The previous Sunday, I had decided to go to church. I needed some time with God in His dwelling again. The pace we set was like running a marathon, weeks flew by. I scoured the internet for nondenominational churches in the area, deciding on Weatherstone Church in Berlin, Wisconsin. Again, Andrew Coffield and I, along with our incredible leader, Stuart Jolly, went together. Here, I met Pastor Dave Ford who gave one of the best sermons I'd ever experi-enced. Toward the end of the service, Pastor Dave invited those who wanted to come down to the front of the stage for a more personal prayer. While my head was bowed and Pastor Dave was speaking, I felt a tap on the front of my shoulder. I opened my eyes to find Pastor Dave looking at me and he said softly, "I'm glad you're here." He had noticed my Trump staff pin on my lapel. As the service ended, he came down off the stage and shook my hand and thanked me for what I was doing. Stuart and Andrew had come over at that point and I introduced my friends. Pastor Dave was so gracious and appre-ciative, telling us subtly how much he loved Trump. He then took the time to pray for us all, that we would be successful. It was awe-some. Praise the Lord!

Fast forward a week—Easter Sunday. I decided to go back to Weatherstone Church for Pastor Dave's Easter sermon—an even more inspiring experience. This time, I rounded up five of us, includ-ing Josh Whitehouse who hadn't been to church for two years, as I recall. It was time to thank the Lord for what He was doing in our lives and in our country. As we were sitting all in a row, I got a tap on my left shoulder. I turned and found Pastor Dave giving me a big smile and welcome. I introduced my friends and associates, and PD, as I grew to call him, thanked them all for coming. He asked me if I minded if he called us out during the service to which my response was "Absolutely not." A few minutes into the service, Pastor Dave then introduced us all to the congregation. *Sid and the boys from the Trump campaign* are joining us here today. To which we got a rousing applause as we stood and waved. Man, it was one of the highlights of the campaign. What an honor. At the end of the service, PD came up to our aisle. We got in a circle, arms on each other's shoulders leaning in, and he proceeded to say a beautiful prayer for all of us. It reminded me again of how blessed I was to be where the Lord had put me. Five of us went to a nice restaurant for Easter dinner. It wasn't home, but we had become family.

Show horses and workhorses, terms I was quickly learning the meaning of as we crossed the country. Most on our team were workhorses, but there were a couple who weren't and I didn't mind calling you out if you were a show horse. One particular day, we received a delivery of yard sign stakes via tractor trailer. There were two pallets of them and each box weighed about fifty pounds. Their dimensions were about thirty-six inches by thirty-six inches by six inches, flat and awkward to carry. The elevator was broken so we had no choice but to carry each box down the spiral staircase and into the back of the office. We were also joined in Wisconsin by Trump Midwest Regional Director Stephanie Milligan. Stephanie was a very dynamic woman and leader who came in to oversee our operation as we were now in her territory. She was definitely a workhorse and not a show horse. When the truck arrived, there were only a handful of us in the Milwaukee campaign office, one of them being our *IT* staffer Jonathan Dimock. We all dawned what outerwear we had and headed upstairs, including Stephanie in high heels.

I had noticed Dimock sending a text as were about to go out. No sooner did we get upstairs and Dimock's cell phone rang. He gives us the *I'll be right back index* finger and walks down the hallway. The rest of us continue our trek down and up, up and down box by box. After about five minutes, I sternly said "Jonathan, let's go," as he was within sight of all of us. Another five minutes and now I yelled at him to get off the damn phone and help us. This SOB waited until there were just a few boxes left, and then his phone call ended. I was livid! I let him know how I felt, and also Stephanie, telling her if it was up to me I'd send him home. Dimock continued on through the campaign, although after that incident, Matt split us up as we continued on to other states. I lost all respect for this guy, and it was best to keep him away from me. We were all working too hard to accept a slacker on the team. From there, I deemed him just what he was—a professional slacker. A person who knows how to turn it on when it benefits him and slack off when he can get away with it. He never should've been brought forward.

The weather in Wisconsin seemed similar to home—you never knew what to expect. Some days were very cold, windy, and some snow. My three stalwarts, Jason Squeglia, Charles Bruckerhoff, and Robert Bowes, were just incredible guys and awesome team leaders. There were others, of course, but these three would run circles around most and would have their teams out the door, knocking for ten straight hours most days. The incredible thing was that they were such great leaders and communicators that their teams of volunteers didn't mind. Each of these three would later come on board as Trump staff, but at this point were still *super volunteers* away from home to help our cause, and I loved each of them for it. People in Wisconsin seemed to either love Mr. Trump or hate him. Some even yelled and swore at our door knockers. One even sicced their dog on staffer Josh Whitehouse. To hear the story of Josh running to the SUV to escape his near fate was hilarious. It was also here that we found one of the most astute and hardest workers I'd met on the campaign. A young man showed up one day to volunteer—tall, slender, and only twenty years old. He was quiet and didn't know much about politics, except that he and his family loved Mr. Trump.

His name was Aleks Urosevic, a Serbian from Milwaukee. Aleks would drive an hour each way just to come and volunteer with us door knocking. Charles took him under his wing and on his team. Aleks was a student in between studies and had the time to help us. We came to find out that there was a very large Serbian population in Wisconsin who all loved Mr. Trump. Aleks would show up in the morning, knock doors all day until early evening, then stay to help phone bank until about nine at night before he'd depart for home. Charles would tell us how terrific Aleks was at the doors, speaking with people about Mr. Trump's agenda to make America great again. He was one the most mature twenty-year-olds I'd ever met, as well as just a great person. We all took a very strong liking to Aleks, and as we wound down in Wisconsin, he asked us if we needed help going forward. One of our other staffers from Ohio, Andrew Coffield, offered to share a hotel room if Aleks could be brought forward. Andrew saw how extraordinary and dedicated Aleks was and knew he'd be a great addition to our Strike Team. I got it approved, no pay, but we'd cover his hotel and food and that's all he needed. His family was so proud of him. I didn't know it then, but the Lord had again blessed me with another wonderful friend.

Nancy Mace was doing her thing running the Appleton office, although not a lot changed. I was getting calls from some staff griping about the way they were being treated. One of them, Jay Aubin who had been with us since New Hampshire, was telling me he was going home to North Carolina if he had to be on her team again. I'd later find out about all kinds of shenanigans that went on up there near Green Bay. Nancy had been her usual antagonistic self, but we still made the impact we wanted. We lost to Ted Cruz by about 18 percent but still took second place and gained more delegates. We all headed home to our families for a much needed break. It was here I said goodbye to my dear friend Charles Bruckerhoff who was going home to Connecticut. Charles needed to get back to helping his wife run their business, and I was heartbroken saying goodbye to him. We had been together since December in New Hampshire, and we truly admired and respected each other. I was losing one of my best team leaders who I always counted on, but more importantly, I was losing my dear friend temporarily. It would be months before I'd see him again along the campaign trail. We clearly made an impression in Wisconsin, as was seen in the general election to come.

Charles door knocking in Wisconsin

County map of Indiana. One of many maps I worked
with to identify where we needed to "focus" our efforts

Field Director and good friend Stuart Jolly
in Wisconsin. I had to do it

Easter dinner with my "family"
(left to right) Charles, Ben, Robert, me and Andrew

Sharing objectives with new volunteers

Mid-West Director Stephanie Milligan at the office in
Mineminee Falls Wisconsin. Open House night

My office in Wisconsin. My walls were plastered with maps

My strength

Wisconsin was one of my most favorite offices

CHAPTER 11

The Biggest Win Yet—Indiana

We all flew home for a well needed break—almost two full days—then off to Indianapolis. Fortunately, most of the offices had been prearranged for us. We set up in Carmel, just north of Indy. Others offices were in Evansville and Fort Wayne. Later, we decided to open another in the northwest corner of the state in Lake County. We loved Indiana, and they loved Mr. Trump. The weather was warmer as spring was getting close and it was great door knocking weather, most of the time. It seemed as though rarely, if ever, were all the offices ideally suited to campaign out of. The office in Carmel was previously a pizza restaurant found by someone in the Indiana GOP. It was ridiculously small with tile floors and no office space to work out of. We worked behind a wall where the ovens had been, and we crammed signs, stakes, and everything else into a tiny back room. Our U-Haul arrived, and we unloaded what we needed for tables, chairs, signs, and office material. Then off it went to the other offices. We had some incredible staff and volunteers who were extremely dedicated to doing whatever it took.

Indiana gave us two of the best state staff I'd worked with. State Director Suzie Jaworowski and Deputy State Director Cody Reynolds. Both were new to their positions and looked to us for direction of what to do and how to do it. We jelled tremendously and became a very dynamic team quickly. Cody new Indiana politics very well and was extremely knowledgeable in terms of where to focus our efforts. He and I would review the most important counties and towns which surrounded each office, and then I'd work with New York to upload this information into an app format. These would be in dozens of codes which I would then email to each office, and from there, dispersed to the respective door knocking teams. I would perform this task every day. We began our open house events in each office and were deluged by people wanting to volunteer. Our office in Carmel was so small you could barely hear yourself think. The poor phone bankers had to struggle to hear but they made it work. I had Jason Squeglia, who was becoming my best friend, with me in Carmel. We'd get to the office by about 7:30 every morning, and go over our plan for teams and team leaders for each day.

I turned sixty years old in Indiana, and some of the gang took me out for a birthday dinner at about 9:30 one night. It felt great and I appreciated the love from the guys. I tried not to think about missing home and how Denise would've loved having a sixtieth birthday party for me. But we all were making sacrifices, and this was small compared to the one Mr. Trump was making. The left wing media was doing their best to tear him down but he never faltered, and we weren't about to, either. On occasion, they'd pull Jason for motorcade duty when Mr. Trump would come to town and I'd be infuriated. He was the best at it and well trusted by all of Mr. Trump's staff. I just didn't want to sacrifice my best guy for a day, but he loved doing it just as I used to and I would concede. In reality, I hardly had a choice. This is also where our Serbian volunteer, Aleks Urosevic, came into his own. Aleks was proving to be much more than we ever expected. Mature, articulate, and dependable. He was up to any challenge, so I started putting him into a team leader role. It rankled a few older staffers who were sent in from other states to assist us, but he deserved the chance. And in most cases, he was both more mature and harder working than them so I didn't care whether they liked it or not. I made it very clear that his direction was to be taken as though it was coming from me.

Another young talent who joined us from Ohio was Andrew Coffield. Andrew was in his mid-twenties and previously on staff in that state. He also began taking on a more responsible role in our day-to-day efforts and another person we could count on for anything. We were sending out hundreds of volunteers door knocking every day from each office and knocking on tens of thousands of doors to get information. We'd try to persuade voters who might be on the fence as to why they should vote for Mr. Trump. On April 18, it felt like things were beginning to unravel. We heard on the news that our field director and highly respected leader Stuart Jolly had resigned. There was a top staff reorganization going on which we were not aware of. Paul Manafort was hired by Mr. Trump, and Rick Wiley was a Manafort guy from their past. Stuart was not going to report to Wiley and quickly resigned. We were devastated as there was talk that Manafort and Wiley would simply dismantle the Strike Team. Aleks and Andrew came to me Tuesday morning, brought forward by Jason. They were completely distressed over our future. I took them outside the back of the office as this was not something to discuss in front of volunteers who were beginning to arrive.

I needed to quell their anxiety. Jason and I began by impressing upon them that we still had a job to do, regardless. And until we were told something different, we needed to focus on that responsibility. I told them that it was very unlikely that we would be disbanded as we were a very necessary force and were making a difference. "It was out of our control, so let's focus on what is in our control until we hear differently." I assured them that everything was going to be alright, and how much I needed them to not lose their focus on the job at hand. They came around quickly and performed as the professionals they were. I called Stuart later in the morning to find out what was going on. He explained his feelings toward Wiley from knowledge of his past and I had to respect his decision, as difficult as it was. He encouraged me to stay the course and everything would be okay. When I pressed him for the skinny on Wiley, he simply pointed out how Rick Wiley *will never know your wife's name.* In other words, he's all business and nothing more. We were used to that personal touch and caring that we got from Stuart. He was the best person I'd ever reported to and I was deeply saddened to see him leave. As I told my guys, we had a mission to complete and we pressed on.

A few days after Stuart departed, into the Carmel office came Rick Wiley, backpack in tow, and introduced himself to everyone. He certainly seemed like a nice guy in the short time I knew him. Paul Manafort had been hired by Mr. Trump personally and we were not sure what this meant in terms of who was going to be calling the shots, he or Corey Lewandowski. We had been hearing rumblings that the family was getting tired of Corey's ways, but we also knew Corey was well-liked by Mr. Trump. With the primaries heading to a close and us leading the pack, Manafort was brought on due to his political expertise. His background was lawyer, lobbyist, and political consultant. He was previously an advisor to the presidential campaigns of Gerald Ford, Ronald Reagan, George H.W. Bush, and Bob Dole. Corey had never run a national campaign and there were doubts that he could pull off a win in the general election against Hillary Clinton.

Each day, we had a conference call with all state campaign offices. Stephanie Milligan would lead it off and address the latest headlines and remind us all to stay focused. Matt Ciepielowski would address phone banking numbers, and then I'd address the previous day's state door knocking numbers and current goals. We were nailing our numbers and knocking on tens of thousands of doors. The media kept up their leftist slant of bashing our campaign and stating that Trump didn't have much of a ground game. We knew differently and would prove them all wrong. Most nights, I'd get back to my hotel room by around ten o'clock and work until nearly midnight. Every night, I would send out a report reflecting that day's achievements of houses reached. Along with that was a motivational statement to everyone on our team. Quotes from some of the greatest and most courageous people throughout history, i.e., Winston Churchill, General Patton, General MacArthur, President Reagan, and even a couple from our beloved leader Mr. Trump that went like this:

"Without passion you don't have energy, without energy you have nothing. Sometimes by losing a battle you find a new way to win the war."

Yes, we had lost some battles along the way but we were winning the war, so to speak. The liberal media was having a heart attack.

There were few polls which were accurate, except perhaps the Fox News polls. We rarely were losing by what the media was saying, and we always won by more as well. They couldn't help themselves, and Mr. Trump played them like a violin. We tore through Indiana like the tornado I nearly drove through on my way back to the hotel one night. It was late and I was driving from Carmel to my hotel room just south of Indianapolis with warnings of possible tornados popping up. As I got closer to the Indy airport, the sky was as black as could be and the wind was picking up. Then it started to downpour. That quickly turned into a heavy hailstorm. Within five minutes, I was driving into torrential rain mixed with large hail balls driven sideways by the wind. It sounded like my SUV was being hit by a machine gun. The wind was so strong I struggled to stay in my lane; visibility was zero. What I didn't anticipate was cars in front of me were not just slowing down, they were all stopped under a bridge. I swerved at the last second, just barely missing a collision. If there was a tornado nearby, I knew enough that sitting under a bridge was not a good idea, so I kept going. By the grace of God, I made it to my hotel safely. Relieved was an understatement. Growing up in the Northeast, I was accustomed to driving in blizzards, heavy rain, and wind. Nothing much ever scared me while driving, until this night.

A particularly fond memory and example of God-loving Trump supporters happened on a Monday after a very busy weekend. One of the staff from Alabama who was there to assist had rented a cotton candy machine for the supporters pouring through the Carmel office that weekend. I needed to get some supplies and agreed to return the unit to the rental company. When I was driving back after dropping it off, I saw a Waffle House nearby and decided to swing in for a quick bite as it was late morning. I sat at the end of the counter next to a large booth. A family of townies came in with friends and kids, and all sat in this booth next to me. It wasn't long before they were talking about Mr. Trump's recent visit to the state and how they loved him. These were blue-collar folks who looked like they were taking a break from their farm. They said something which prompted me to interject. One pointed out my Bostonian accent which led me to inform them of why I was in their state. I told them I ran the ground campaign for Mr. Trump, and after some questions and dialog, they all thanked me profusely for my efforts. They went back to their discussion, and I went back to reviewing things in my phone. Ten minutes later, I asked for my check whereupon the waitress told me I was all set. I was puzzled. I hadn't paid yet. She pointed to the booth and whispered, "They took care of it." Strangers who I didn't even know had paid for my meal. Again, there I was being thankful and humbled by where God had put me.

Indiana put the finishing touches on Mr. Trump being the presumptive Republican nominee. We attended a Republican watch party the night of the primary. It was sponsored by a great Republican and even greater American, Rex Early from Indiana. There were hundreds of people there and big screens all around, food and drinks for all. We watched the numbers coming in with great anticipation. Then it was announced, "Trump wins Indiana!" This was our greatest win yet and the first major goal we wanted to attain—getting Mr. Trump on his way to the general election. State Director Suzie Jaworowski came over to me and we hugged each other. I couldn't help crying, and neither could she. We had worked side by side thirteen to sixteen hours every day for weeks, making it happen. We shared family problems along with happy times which we each struggled with while being away from our families. My son Brandon and his wife Mara had their firstborn while I was in Indiana—my new granddaughter MacKenzie. Suzie had given me a hug during a teary happy moment days earlier, as I was sad I couldn't go to California to see her. We even struggled to unplug toilets together in the campaign office as there were plumbing issues. We had become very good friends. Suzie and her husband Steve had our team, along with our number one Indiana volunteer Jacquie, to their home for a rare Sunday early evening cookout. At last, some home-cooked food prepared primarily by Steve. It was awesome and so appreciated.

My now dear friend Jason and I hugged and proclaimed to each other, *"We did it!"* After all the congratulations were done, we were ready to leave the event. Before we left, Jacquie and her husband Dave gathered us in a circle. Arms on shoulders and heads bowed, Dave said a beautiful prayer asking the Lord to bless us going forward and keep us safe. These were some of the most memorable moments on the campaign trail for me. I was in awe at the level of care and love directed to us during our travels, as well as the commitment to our effort by the thousands of volunteers. Jason, Aleks Urosevic, Andrew Coffield, and I went out for a bite to eat. During our meal and watching the election news on television, there came another moment of great news. Ted Cruz drops out of the race! We won all fifty-seven delegates for Indiana which put us over the top. Mr. Trump was the last one standing in the Republican primary. Eleven months of very hard work had paid off. Not once did I ever doubt that Mr. Trump wouldn't win. God placed his soldiers where He needed us, and we persevered with His guidance. That being said, we still needed as many more delegates as possible as the next fight would be from within—the Republican Convention.

Leaving Indiana. Jason never traveled light

Andrew Coffied and Aleks Urosevic meeting us at the Carmel
Indiana Campaign Office. We just came from church

Enjoying a home cooked meal at Indiana State Director
Suzie Jaworowski's house late Sunday afternoon

These guys knew how to get it done

Indiana State Director and great friend Suzie Jaworowski

Jason and I celebrating in Indiana

(left to right) Jason Squeglia, me, Aleks Urosevic,
Joe Forkin and Andrew Coffield

NH staffer and Strike Team member Danny Tiso
loaded and leaving for Nebraska next

One of the best tattoos I saw in our travels

Team members taking me out on my 60th birthday in Indiana

CHAPTER 12

Nebraska and California—the Last Two Stops

We were in Indiana for nearly a month and all flew straight to Nebraska. The dismantling of the strike team never occurred. It was decided by still Campaign Manager Corey Lewandowski to send us to Nebraska and California to persuade as many voters as possible to vote for Mr. Trump. We still needed to acquire as many delegates as possible to assure a win within our party. There were a lot of disgruntled Republican delegates who supported other candidates who did not like Mr. Trump. We flew out of Indiana all with the same destination—Omaha, Nebraska. It was here that the wheels on the Nancy Mace wagon began to fall off. While in Nebraska, I had one of the young *super volunteers* who had jumped on our team come to me and practically beg me to not keep putting him out with her. Omaha was our only campaign office, and therefore we worked under one roof. Nancy started her crap almost immediately. She had somehow gotten her hands on some of the codes for door knocking, pulled together *her* team, and off she was going to knock on doors.

Since I had just walked in the Omaha office shortly after I had checked into our hotel, I hadn't had time to distribute them. By her just randomly plucking some codes and not communicating with me, there would be a chance that I'd then send a team to the same area. I confronted her outside and told her to follow protocol. She was a woman on a mission. The problem was she was just too headstrong and wouldn't take direction. Brash and irrational, she was disliked by many on the team. We only had a week to do what we could in Nebraska. We sent out email blasts and had a good showing of volunteers, although many were confused as to why we were there considering Ted Cruz had dropped out. We had phone bankers and plenty of door knockers but not quite the same level of intensity. It felt like we had gone twelve rounds of boxing, won a title fight, but needed to keep shadowboxing after we won.

A few days before the primary, I witnessed God's love again. One of the kindest examples of love and friendship I'd ever seen. We all knew we would be heading for California next. Aleks Urosevic came to me and asked if he could continue on with us. He wasn't on staff and the answer would have to be no. He had been with us since Wisconsin, and as mentioned, was a great volunteer, a great person, and well-liked by everyone. I would have loved to have brought him but it was an airfare expense that wasn't necessary. He had resigned himself to taking a bus from Omaha back to Wisconsin in a few days and I was saddened at the thought of saying goodbye. I asked Aleks to come up to my hotel room one night as I had something for him. When he arrived, we sat and reflected about the past couple of months. I told him what an exceptional person he was. He was a devout Christian and firmly believed in the plan—His plan. We talked about his exceptional contribution to the campaign, and I thanked him for everything he had done to help us.

In recognition for all he had done and what he meant to me, I handed him a coveted Trump staff pin as a memento for being with us. It was quite a moment as he held it and put his arms around me and thanked me. I loved this kid and told him so. He was a special person, and off he went. The next day I witnessed the Lord's grace. Andrew Coffield came to me asking for a private conversation. He asked me, "If someone paid for Aleks's airfare to California, could we take him along?" He then offered to share his hotel room if we could bring him. That *someone* was him—Andrew. He really liked Aleks and felt he deserved to continue on and would pay for the ticket himself, but did not want Aleks to know who paid for it. My answer was yes, whereupon he asked me to keep it as an anonymous donor.

The ticket was over $500. It was one of the kindest and most generous acts I've ever witnessed. Aleks was elated when I told him he'd be coming to California and continue his journey with us. Naturally, he wanted to know who but respected that I was sworn to secrecy. We won all thirty-six delegates to be had in Nebraska, and left Omaha on May eleventh with our heads held high.

We all headed home for a quick break, hardly long enough for a few good meals and a kiss from Denise. Without children living at home and two cats who didn't make much noise, it had been a long haul for her—most nights eating alone and many cold winter days needing to do everything herself. We missed each other terribly, and she was never anything but wonderful. Most days I hardly had five minutes to talk with her as there just wasn't time. There was never a moment of *There, I'm all done.* Days had blended into weeks and weeks into months and she never griped once. Well, maybe once. I would call her every night, but the further West we went the time difference made it more difficult. She was lonely and missed me while trying to keep busy as best as possible. But our faith never wavered, and we simply knew that we had to do this together. I was again home for a day and a half, then gone to connect with my team in sunny liberal California.

Matt and I had scheduled three quarters of the team into Southern California. We landed in Irvine and I had booked us at the Hilton. Andrew Coffield and Aleks Urosevic flew into Sacramento. Nancy Mace, Ohio State Director Rob Scott, and a handful of the younger staff and volunteers flew into San Diego. Then a couple of other state directors flew into San Francisco. The good thing was these offices were all prearranged for us by California State Director Tim Clark. I also had arranged hotels for all the others, as well as several SUVs. Mr. Trump had picked up the entire tab on every expense from day one. He paid for tens of thousands of dollars in hotels, rental vehicles, the RVs, U-Hauls, and food for us and the volunteers in every office. At one point, I recall adding it all up and it was well in excess of a million dollars just for our strike team. In total, he had racked up over fifty million dollars out of his own pocket and it wasn't over yet. We all loved this man for what he was willing to sacrifice to help save our country.

I immediately began working with Tim Clark to review our pre-arranged areas of coverage for the ground campaign. Matt and Josh Whitehouse began working on email blasts to pull in volunteers to each office. Surprisingly, there were thousands of Republican volunteers in California and they poured into every office to phone bank and knock doors with us. I kept each office moving by providing all the door knocking codes and coordinates of where we needed to focus our ground campaign, continuing to pull those on the fence over to vote for Mr. Trump. As we traveled around Southern California, you couldn't help but be appalled at the homeless situation. There were virtually thousands of permanent tent cities spread out around the entire state. Los Angeles, Hollywood, Long Beach, and even Beverly Hills. Along sidewalks, under overpasses, and along street blocks, this once wealthy state has succumbed to its die-hard Democrat rule and Liberal policies. Taxes have skyrocketed and regulations have stifled small business creation. Illegal immigration has exploded here. Governor Jerry Brown has declared California a sanctuary state for goodness sake. The mandatory $15/hour minimum wage has hurt low income workers because retail businesses are moving more to automation to save money. California's public pension systems are about $200 billion in the red.

The California GOP had an office in Whittier, and we needed to have more presence in that part of Southern California. So I took my now good friend Jason Squeglia with me, and we packed up and left Irvine for Whittier. We stayed in the Double Tree by Hilton for the better part of three weeks. Right around this time, Mr. Trump began coming into California quite a bit. Things were getting ugly at this point when the boss came to an event. The tolerant left had become not so tolerant and protesters became violent upon Mr. Trump's arrival. Fortunately, that was right before we arrived but we'd soon enough see it for ourselves. Jason had been selected to drive in the motorcades from state to state when Mr. Trump came in for a rally.

Because our tempo and intensity had slowed down a bit as this was the last state and primary to be held, I had more time than any time over the past several months to perform other tasks. Therefore, I assisted Jason as the number two staff car for nearly all the motorcades moving Mr. Trump around California. Mr. Trump has a home in Beverley Hills and he resided there for the last couple of weeks before the primary. Jason and I each had black Chevy Suburban which I arranged ahead of time as we knew this was coming. It was an honor and one of the most exciting things I've ever done. Even though I had driven in many motorcades in New Hampshire, there wasn't the intensity that revolved around the campaign now. Secret Service was heavily involved, and considering the danger from the left wing whack jobs in California, security was beefed up more than ever.

I kept my laptop with me and worked on the ground campaign every chance I had when we were parked, waiting at a rally, or while waiting for Mr. Trump to land at the L.A. airport. Jason and I lived in those Suburbans for the better part of two weeks. If Mr. Trump wasn't doing a rally, then we were driving him to different fund-raising events. One day, the entire motorcade pulled into the back of the building where the Jimmy Kimmel Show is aired in Hollywood. Mr. Trump was doing a guest appearance and while we waited out back, there were four police helicopters circling overhead the entire time. Secret Service and police armed with M-16 machine guns were everywhere, including rooftops. I'll always remember the people along Sunset Boulevard cheering for Mr. Trump as we came along. It was awesome to see the support, even in California.

One constant for our motorcade was the California Highway Patrol, or CHIPs as they were known. These men were absolute heroes in every sense. The first time Jason and I encountered them was when picking up Mr. Trump and his staff at LAX, Los Angeles International Airport. There were about twenty-five motorcycles parked at the private pick-up side of the airport. As was typical protocol, we arrived two hours before wheels down/arrival time. Two SUVs had five heavily armed SWAT police in each, night vision on helmets, and all with machine guns. Fifteen minutes before Mr.

Trump's Boeing 757 lands, we all pull out onto the tarmac, just like we did back in New Hampshire. We line up side by side in the order we'll travel in. Mr. Trump's plane lands and slowly pulls up close to where we are. I always took the liberty to take a short video and pictures. It was an experience of a lifetime. As the engines wound down, we'd begin our circle of the plane and come around to the stairs.

First off, the plane were Secret Service agents armed with M-16s who were traveling with Mr. Trump. Jason and I would get out of our Suburbans and open our doors; you never knew who was getting into your vehicle. Quite often, it was Corey Lewandowski, Keith Schiller, Michael Glassner, Dan Scavino, Hope Hicks, or others. Jason and I knew them all pretty well as we'd been around them for several months now. They were all absolutely great people. There were others, too, who had begun traveling with the campaign who we didn't know as well. They were always friendly and chatty to us as we were part of the team, and they always expressed their gratitude to us for what we did. They knew we were in the trenches, so to speak, and were aware of everything Jason and I did. They made a point to always recognize our dedication. They would throw their luggage in the back of our SUVs quickly, and as soon as Mr. Trump's door closed in the second vehicle, the motorcade moved out. The CHIPs would take the lead out of LAX, stopping traffic at all lights and intersections as we headed for the highway.

Blue lights blazing, the motorcade picked up speed. This was serious stuff, and we had be alert and focused. The CHIPs would move ahead and literally close down the highway behind where our on-ramp would enter onto it. Six lanes stopped while we barreled onto the highway. There wasn't a car in sight in front of us as we traveled along at about seventy miles per hour. The police motorcycles were in front, beside us, and taking up the rear. As we got close to our exit, half of the motorcycles would zoom ahead in order to block intersections, and I'm sure scout for danger of any kind. As we traveled along main roads, motorcycle after motorcycle would zoom past my SUV. They'd stop their bikes to block cars, then jump back on and accelerate back up to the motorcade. They did this day and night, putting their lives at risk to perform their task of protection. It was incredibly dangerous and such an honor to be part of it.

Most nights we would bring Mr. Trump back to his house around eleven to twelve o'clock, then bring Corey and the rest of the staff to the Beverley Hills Marriott. We then had a solid hour's drive back to our hotel in Whittier. Jason and I would literally get about two hours of sleep some nights as we needed to be back at his home by 4:30 a.m. per Secret Service. We'd get there and wait for all vehicles to arrive, bomb sweep again, and then wait for the staff to arrive via Uber. We couldn't go and pick them up because, after vehicles were bomb swept, you couldn't leave sight of the Secret Service. Usually by about eight o'clock, Mr. Trump and Keith Schiller, his bodyguard, would come out and be ready to go. The streets around Mr. Trump's house were all blocked off with Beverley Hills police vehicles positioned 24/7. There also was an armored SWAT vehicle and team stationed there 24/7, armed to the teeth. At this point, Mr. Trump had a few of his closest friends joining us. Many times, I had now Secretary of the Treasury Steve Mnuchin sitting next to me in the passenger's seat. Another was Arizona State Treasurer Jeff DeWit. Both were just regular guys, very friendly and congenial. They both thanked me for my contribution when they found out I had run the ground campaign across the country for Mr. Trump.

We drove *The Boss* all over Southern California. It was either to fund-raisers, a rally, or to the airport if he was flying off to a rally elsewhere. One of the fund-raisers was in a large mansion. Shortly after we arrived, Jason and I were requested to come in for a bite to eat. We sat and dined with Political Director Michael Glassner and others. I can assure you, Hillary Clinton would never have done this. As a matter of fact, we had heard stories from some of the Secret Service guys who had friends in the service that were attached for her protection—story after story of how horrible she treated the Secret Service agents and we were told they disliked her tremendously. She was foulmouthed and nasty. What a surprise. On the other hand, they loved Mr. Trump. He treated everyone with respect. The days were long but the excitement was energizing. One morning, we left Mr. Trump's home and headed for LAX. Mr. Trump was flying up to

Fresno for a rally. When he was done there, he was flying directly to San Diego for another rally. When the 757's wheels were up, Jason and I started our three-hour drive to San Diego.

Protocol had us there two hours before he would land for another bomb sweep, and then parked on the tarmac right next to the runway. We could see the city lines, as well as an aircraft carrier in the bay off in the distance. Soon, we'd see the big Boeing 757 with the big *T* on the tail coming down. What a sight! I never got tired of that big bird heading over to us and parking right next to us. I took lots of great pictures and videos there as well. The plane stopped, and we circled it to the other side. Secret Service out first, staff, and then Mr. Trump and off we went. We motorcaded to the rally point and came through back roads to avoid all the crazy protesters. You know, all those peaceful, loving, and tolerant but violent liberals. We pulled inside a large overhead door which closed behind us. We were still outside but had a large concrete wall surrounding us. There in front of us was a very large armored SWAT vehicle and about twelve heavily armed men in full combat gear. Some even had shotguns with additional ammo wrapped around their bodies. Shortly after Mr. Trump entered the building to blaring music and a screaming crowd, these guys went out that overhead door. Most were standing on the outside of the vehicle, heading out to confront the violence. It was incredible to be part of all this, and Jason and I were in our element.

Another night, I remember clearly was the night Jason peeled off from the motorcade. Protocol was you follow the vehicle in front of you. The motorcade was heading back to Beverley Hills when all of a sudden Jason turned right, out of the line. I followed, and we ended up at the Marriott. The Secret Service and police behind me continued on with the motorcade. I came to find out, Corey had told Jason to drop them off instead of going all the way to Mr. Trump's house, and then back to the Marriott as we'd been doing. The next morning, the head of the California Secret Service came up to us and quite sternly asked why the hell we pulled out of the motorcade. Jason pointed out that he was told by the Campaign Manager Corey Lewindowski to take the turn. He went on to tell us to never do that again no matter who tells us to and that he'd address it with Corey.

He then handed us each an American flag pin but not just any pin. This one had the Secret Service emblem in the flag as he thanked us for our service. What an honor. He explained that nearly every four years during a presidential election, at least one motorcycle officer loses his life doing his job. He pointed out that if one of these guys was coming up on the right and not aware we were turning, he could be killed.

You can only imagine how guilty Jason felt the next night—same route and same scenario. Corey told Jason to take the turn but this time Jason voiced that he was told not to. Corey then told him in no uncertain terms that he was the campaign manager not the Secret Service and to make the turn. This time, as Jason turned out of the motorcade while we're going about forty miles per hour, I started to say "No, no, no!" out loud. My fellow staffers all asked what was wrong, so I explained. I stayed in line this time and closed the gap to the vehicle in front of me. We continued on and brought Mr. Trump to his house, then I headed for the Marriott to drop off those in my Suburban. Jason and I hooked up, refueled, and headed for Whittier at about 12:30 a.m. We never heard another thing about it from anyone but we knew the shit hit the fan somehow. We got into our hotel rooms about 1:30 a.m., slept for almost two hours, showered, got back into suit and ties, and back to Beverley Hills at about 80 mph. In between all of this, I somehow managed to continue to send out door knocking codes to the other offices with some help from Matt Ciepielowski.

One night while waiting at the Los Angeles airport for Mr. Trump to return from another state, I received a call from one of my fellow New Hampshire staffers, Danny Tiso. Danny was part of our strike team when we left New Hampshire. Nineteen years old, sharp, and a great kid. Poor Danny was put on Nancy Mace's team in San Diego and couldn't take it anymore. He called me, pleading for me to pull him out of San Diego and bring him up to the L.A. area with us. He started telling his reasons why. According to Danny, Nancy and Ohio State Director Rob Scott had been drinking heavily night in and night out with all the staff there, some who were underage. He reported that Nancy had been fudging the numbers to make it appear they had done much more than they actually did and were told not to say anything. I wasn't a bit surprised since I knew she was the type of person who would do nearly anything to make herself look better than others. I called Matt—as Matt was the strike team leader—and he agreed that we should pull Danny out of there.

Nancy was irate that we pulled one of her team away, and I explained that he'd had enough of her condescending treatment as she did to all of the staff under her. What was going on there was a recipe for a media disaster and I took it upon myself to let her know. Danny had also shared a couple of Snapchats between Nancy and Rob about me which they also shared with their team down there. The dialog was vulgar and nasty. Not a smart move, as most of the staff had little respect for either of them. Enough was enough, and I proceeded to write a letter to both her and Rob Scott, copying Matt Ciepielowski and Midwest Director Stephanie Milligan. Below is a copy of that letter:

> Nancy and Rob,
>
> There comes a point in time when extremely unprofessional behavior just can't be ignored. For the benefit of the California campaign, I waited until the end to send this. Let's begin with your email last week, Rob, stating, 'Hey, where's the daily numbers? Nancy's team killed it in San Diego.' My response was simple. 'I don't break the daily numbers down individually for a reason. There are too many variables which may impact each office daily so to single out any one office for doing better than others is not fair. We're here as a team and it's a team effort along with a team goal and that's to win every state for Mr. Trump. Please keep in mind there is no *I* in *team*.' A response you both clearly did not like, even though it was very reasonable to everyone except you.

Your response to my email was disturbing, to say the least. A copy of your Snapchat which also went to the young staff and volunteers in your office is included. Not only does it show your continued self-serving nature, it's extremely unprofessional. Rob, for a state director to send something out publicly like this says everything about your judgment and character along with your bad attitude. Nancy, you're here for the wrong reason. This campaign is not about you. Your continued attempts to whip people into place that you direct have made five people state that if they had to be on your team again they would just as soon go home. That's why you've been left with the younger group. Anyone who has been around the block can't tolerate your belittling management style. Your comment of 'he won't share how much the other offices suck' says everything about your lack of team spirit and self-serving negative attitude toward others who disagree with you. And sharing this through a form of social media with younger impressionable staff is inexcusable, unprofessional, and distasteful, to say the least.

It needs to also be mentioned that while here, you have purchased alcohol for underage staff and solicited underage drinking with staff and volunteers in your hotel room. Something which has been going on in previous states as well. This is a recipe for embarrassment to the campaign. I have proof if you'd like to argue this point. I'm quite sure Corey, Michael, and even more so, Mr. Trump would find your actions and behavior inexcusable enough to say those two magic words. Therefore, to the other managers copied on this, it is my profound recommendation that after this campaign, you both are *not* to be brought forward in any capacity as you have proven you don't belong on this *team*. *We* are here to win a presidential campaign, none of us have time to deal with this bullshit going forward in the general.

Sincerely,
Sid Bowdidge

Since I waited until we were wrapped up in California, nothing was done about this at that point. We were all heading home, anyway. The primaries were over. We grabbed all 172 delegates and 75 percent of the Republican vote in California. Next up for us would be the Republican National Convention in July. Nancy and Rob made it there, but that was the end of the road for her. At that point, there was a new sheriff in town—Jim Murphy. Jim had been brought on board as new political director, and we hit it off well. After I shared my email to Nancy and Rob with him, Nancy was left back home in South Carolina and not utilized in the campaign any further. Shortly after this in June, Corey was fired by Mr. Trump. Did these events have anything to do with it? I don't know for sure, but I suspect it didn't help. Corey could be brash and headstrong, but it was he who had gotten us this far. We were shocked and sadly disappointed. He was a good guy and well respected. We'd begun to hear rumblings that some of the family had enough of Corey's antics, especially Ivanka. Corey came from Lowell, Massachusetts, a tough blue-collar city. A place that most don't entirely get out of their system. On top of that, Paul Manafort was now calling the shots. His guy, Rick Wiley, was fired on May 25 by Mr. Trump as well. Apparently, Wiley had a go-round with longtime friend and supporter of Mr. Trump, Karen Giorno, who was also heading up the campaign in Florida. Wiley heard those two magic words, "You're fired."

We had a party the night of June 7 before we left California. The numbers were in, and Mr. Trump was the presumptive Republican nominee. We did what the media and so many said we couldn't do—*we won* the Republican primary! Mr. Trump was the last one standing. What a roller-coaster ride this was. We all packed for home for a much-deserved rest and to prepare for the next battle. Jason and I had grown to love each other like brothers. We had become the best of friends who had the utmost respect and love for each other. I was grabbing a few extra days in Southern California to visit my son Brandon, daughter-in-law Mara, and my new granddaughter. Jason and I had breakfast together on June 8, as we had for months and said goodbye with a hug. The Lord had brought me to a place I could not have ever imagined. An unbelievable journey and I was sad to have it coming to an end, at least this chapter. From my hotel room, I saw Jason in the parking lot putting his suitcases in his Suburban. He then walked over to my vehicle and put something on the windshield. Later, after I checked out, I pulled a piece of paper out from under my windshield wiper. It was a note and it said *I love you, pal. Stay safe*. I couldn't help but to cry as I sat in my Suburban. I was blessed with the best friend a guy could ever ask for. Jason was always looking out for me, doing anything he could to help. He was honest, strong, smart, funny, and generous to everyone. I had never loved a friend like I did this man. I thanked God for putting him in my life. I thanked God for taking me on this incredible journey.

A scene we came across only once as we traveled
the country. No surprise it was California

A unique scene of Cal law enforcement
while we were at a fund raiser

California, I had to do it. There was a Bernie sticker on the front

CHIPS at LAX while we awaited Mr.
Trumps arrival. One of many times

CHIPS lined up outside Mr. Trumps Beverley Hills home

I always teased Jason. He had the cleanest staff car all of the time

Staff watching Intently at a TV monitor for results.
(left to right) George Gigicos, Corey Lewandowski,
Dan Scavino and Michael Glassner

Jason and I out door knocking in sunny Cal

Jason and I out door knocking in sunny Cal

Jason and I were honored to be given these pins
from the California Secret Service Director

Jason at Jimmy Kimmels studio

Jason out of his Staff Car as we dropped of the entourage

Jason Squeglia with Mr. Trump in front of his Citation

Many from our team celebrating our win in Nebraska

Me coming down stairs of Trumps 757

Me door knocking in California

Me outside Jimmy Kimmel's studio waiting
for Mr. Trump to go on his show

My pal Jason ready to go as we awaited
Mr. Trump at the L.A. airport

One of my favorite pics I'd taken of the 757 leaving LAX

One of the many great door knocking teams in California

Outside Mr. Trumps Beverley Hills residence
waiting for a bomb sweep

Overhead shot of the motorcade in San Diego June 2016.
Jason and I are both driving staff cars in this pic

Ready and armed at a Trump rally in San Diego

San Diego skyline as we await Mr. Trumps arrival

San Diego heading out to face the protesters

The big Boeing 757 coming in one night in California

The Boeing 757 approaches our vehicles in California

The consummate professional Jason in his staff car.
He would perform this task all across the country.

Secret Service pin on my left lapel which changed every time we
drove in the motorcade. Right lapel my coveted Trump staff pin

This SWAT team was parked outside Mr.
Trumps house in Beverley Hills 24'7

CHAPTER 13

The Republican National Convention

I came home from California on June 12, 2016. I had only been home for about six days in the past six months, and it felt awkward to wake up and have nothing to do. As strange as it may seem, I missed heading for the next state, I missed the camaraderie, I missed being on a mission. Little did I know that soon enough I would be back to eighty-plus hours a week right to Election Day. After a couple of days' rest, I was back in touch with New Hampshire State Director Matt Ciepielowski. We needed to prepare for the Republican National Convention coming up July 18–21. This wasn't a lock yet, even though Mr. Trump was the presumptive nominee. The convention would solidify our efforts after some arm wrestling in Cleveland. But first, we had to communicate with each of the states' delegates and make sure the majority were going to vote for Trump. I was selected as a whip for Alaska. My task was to call each delegate and feel them out as to who they were voting for. All were Republicans, but not all were on board to cast their vote for Mr. Trump at the RNC. There were still a lot of bitter feelings toward him for the way he had taken down *their* guy. Whether it was *low energy Jeb* or *lying Ted Cruz*, there were many that weren't going to cast their vote for him.

Every single staff member was given a state and delegates to call. I spent hours upon hours talking with delegates in Alaska, and needless to say, the time difference made it difficult. Not only were there delegates but alternates who might need to fill in for a variety of reasons. Most were on board, but several required many conversations in order to help them see the light which, in essence, was a non-vote for Trump was a vote for Clinton. In between, Jason and I did some more motorcading, as Mr. Trump and some staff flew into Boston for a fund-raiser at the Langham Hotel in the Financial District. We suited up and picked up two black Suburbans in Manchester, New Hampshire, and headed for Boston on June 29. The Boston-based Secret Service was there, along with several Massachusetts State Police and motorcycles. After the same routine, two hours before wheels down, we headed into Boston. As we neared, there were about a hundred protesters with signs of all sorts. It was comical. They'd be screaming nasty things and the signs saying *Racist* and such were nonsense. Mr. Trump was the furthest thing from a racist, but they'd all been watching the fake news and drinking the Kool-Aid. Of course, we'd come to discover later on that most of the protesters across the country were in fact paid protesters or just mini Libs who had nothing more important to do in life.

The motorcade pulled down into the basement parking area. We waited for Mr. Trump to have lunch and rub some elbows. They finished, and we headed back to the airport. I had a couple and their daughter get into my Suburban, not having a clue who they were. Very dressed up and very nice people, they had just attended the event and came down with the entourage. They were talking about the event when the wife addressed her husband as *Howie*. It then dawned on me as I recognized the voice, and I asked, "Are you Howie Carr?" "Sure am," he replied. Howie was a famous Boston talk radio figure and I'd listened to him for twenty years off and on. He was always in the Boston limelight and a great guy. His wife and daughter were delightful. I introduced myself and mentioned that I was Mr. Trump's ground campaign manager. They expressed their surprise and asked me some particulars of what I'd done. They thanked me for my service to the campaign, and Howie asked if I'd read any of his books to which I had not but was aware of the content. He handed me his card with his cell number and email, and asked me to send him my address. A few days later, two large envelopes arrived at our house. In them were five of Howie's books, each one with a different note inside and autographed. I was flattered. The motorcade pulled alongside the big 757, and onboard they went with Mr. Trump and the staff who had come along for this trip. Jason and I headed back to New Hampshire. Fortunately, we'd get to do this several more times by the time we got to November 8.

I was helping Matt with different tasks as we plodded through July, as well as continuing my efforts with the Alaskan delegates. On July 17 the New Hampshire strike team all headed to Cleveland for the Republican National Convention, something I'd never experienced. We landed in Cleveland and called for an Uber, cramming several suitcases and six of us into an SUV. As we neared the city, there were two Blackhawk helicopters circling overhead. This was an election unlike any other. The liberal Dems were like rabid animals, they were crazed that Trump was the presumptive nominee and the left wing media only fueled their fire. The country was being torn in half, more divided than ever. I dare say we'd not seen such division and strife since the sixties. We had Hillary Clinton nearly being charged with felony upon felony, only to be let go by FBI Director James Comey. We had DNC employee Seth Rich murdered in DC on July 10—another in the long list of mysterious deaths associated with the Clintons when someone came too close to exposing them for the crooks that they are. The media spent five minutes on this report. Why? Because this poor kid was likely ready to blow the lid on how the Democratic National Committee was fixing their election so Hillary would be the nominee, screwing the old geezer, Bernie Sanders, out of any possibility of winning the nomination. CNN wasn't nicknamed the Clinton News Network for nothing. It was disgraceful, yet business as usual for them.

We all checked into the Westin which was the headquarters for the RNC and Mr. Trump's staff. We received all the clearance badges and schedule we'd need for the week and checked into our rooms. We weren't here for a party, that's for certain. This was ultra-serious stuff. If we didn't or couldn't get enough states to go all in for Mr. Trump, this could turn out to be a disaster. We were scheduled to meet within the belly of the Quicken Loans Arena, downtown Cleveland, on July 18. There were about eighty people in the command center—staff of all levels. The three people running everything were Paul Manafort, Jim Murphy, Brian Jack, and a couple others. We were all given mics so we could communicate trouble areas throughout the arena. The first day was the most challenging as there were multiple competing factions converging at the convention which brought visions of chaos and disorder. The heads of our team were in a bird's nest overseeing what was happening on the floor in each state. Teams were sent in to oversee six states as they tried to force a roll call vote ahead of schedule in the hope of shifting enough support to Ted Cruz to get his name on the ballot. Despite their best efforts to thwart the official nomination of Mr. Trump, it failed, and overall, the convention was an enormous success.

Each day and into the night, I stood in the section of Alaskan Alternates, keeping an eye out for trouble from any liberals who may have snuck in. Mr. Trump came onto the stage the first night to music and an overall rousing applause. It was one of the proudest moments of my life and one of those *pinch me* moments. Night after night, there were great people who spoke, who inspired the crowd, and made us all feel proud to be Americans again. Speakers such as Marcus Luttrell, former United States Navy Seal and American hero. His speech in support of Mr. Trump was inspiring. I met Marcus in a hallway and had the opportunity to thank him for his service and have my picture taken with him. This was one huge human being, physically and in stature. I was honored. Other highlights were meeting renowned broadcast journalist Ted Koppel, best known for being the anchor of Nightline from 1980 until 2005. I also got to meet one of the great college football coaches, Lou Holtz—another proud moment. The area I covered at the arena was just up from the Fox News broadcasting area. At times, I was twenty feet away from Sean Hannity and others. One night, I took the opportunity to sit next to Geraldo Rivera and have my picture taken. Not that this was any great honor, but it was still fun.

Of course, there were the occasional liberal nitwits who managed to get in and stir up some trouble, nearly getting pummeled and be escorted out by the police. One day we arrived early, and while the arena was filling up, out came one of the biggest jackasses of all time, Stephen Colbert. Only a Liberal would do what he did, and of course, only a Liberal could get away with it. He came walking out dressed like Liberace, flamboyant and speaking as though he were a gay man. He wore a brightly colored turban and held a fake white cat in his arms, petting it as he walked around. Television cameras followed him around and he mimicked someone who would be giving a narration on the RNC. Considering he is a devout Progressive Liberal and anti-American piece of crap, I couldn't help but hope someone would trip him, or better yet, punch him in the face. What a low light of the whole event. You would *never* see a Republican do something like this. On the other hand, the absolute highlight of my time in Cleveland was catching up with my dear friend Charles Bruckerhoff.

One of us had texted the other, and then realized we were both there. Charles was a Connecticut delegate, hence his presence at the convention. We met up at the arena and just hugged each other. It was so great to see him. For the duration of the week, we hung out as much as we could, although my days consisted of getting to the arena by late morning and working until we left around midnight each night. So we mostly grabbed breakfast together, and at the end of the convention, I said goodbye to my good friend once again. I got to meet some of the folks from Alaska who I had spent a lot of time with on the phone for weeks before the convention. The final night gave me goose bumps and I had to hold back tears. Ivanka introduced her father as the next President of the United States, and I couldn't have felt more proud for the role we played in getting him to this point. The loud chants of "USA! USA! USA!" rang in my ears like beautiful music. Denise was home watching it, and we texted off and on. I sent her great pictures, but I missed her so much. A year of grueling hours and dedication had finally paid off. We weren't there yet, but we were close. Mr. Trump was now officially the Republican presidential nominee. We'd soon find out our opponent would be Hillary. It was in the bag for her the whole time anyway, as we'd soon find out how the DNC rigged it that way. Poor crazy Bernie, all that time and money spent and he never had a real chance.

The next morning, we were all to fly back to New Hampshire, but there was one small problem. Two days before, Southwest Airlines had a computer glitch that held up flights for a day. They were still recovering and our flights were all on hold with no sure time of departure. I proposed to Matt that we drive home from Cleveland. We could be home in about eleven hours if we drove straight home. He agreed, so I rented the largest SUV I could find and five of us loaded up and off we went. It was a lot of fun with a lot of laughs. We left Cleveland around noontime, and I drove for the first seven hours and then swapped with Josh Whitehouse the rest of the way. We got back to the Trump headquarters around midnight, and then home. What an incredible week and another wonderful experience. Not a day went by without me realizing how blessed I was.

An honor meeting famous college football
coach and Trump supporter Lou Holtz

Charles and I saying hello to infamous author
and Boston talk radio's Howie Carr

Chatting with Geraldo Riveira at the RNC Cleveland

Grabbing a bite at the RNC Convention with great
friends Brent McNeely and Charles Bruckerhoff

Josh Whitehouse taking home a souvenir

Last night of the Republican National Convention. What a night

Matt C. and I at the Convention in Clevevland

Me with US Navy Seal and war hero Marcus Luttrell

Meeting Ted Koppel at the Cleveland Convention

Official RNC tags in order to get into the convention each day

The beginning of a day at the RNC Cleveland

CHAPTER 14

Home at Last

I felt like I had been traveling for a year and had the impression things were going to slow down a bit. There was a bit of a lull while the Republican National Committee, the New Hampshire GOP, and the Trump team figured out how to all work together. Up to this point, we had called all the shots in terms of what, how, and where. All of a sudden, we were not in charge of our destination and the shots would be called by the RNC. Mr. Trump would no longer be picking up the tab, and their leadership team came into play in each state. Speaking for New Hampshire, that wasn't an issue. The RNC team moved into our Trump headquarters and there simply wasn't enough office space, so I soon found myself working out of my home office. The entire New Hampshire staff was then put on the RNC payroll, except me. I had flown down to DC to meet with Trump Political Director Jim Murphy earlier. Because of my position with the campaign, he wanted to keep me on his staff which was more than okay with me.

The night before I went to DC to meet with Jim Murphy, I had a stomachache which felt very similar to the one I had in Wisconsin when I had a bleeding ulcer. I took the same medication I had taken back then, but this time it had no effect. Denise dropped me off at the Manchester airport the next morning and I was feeling worse. I picked up my rental car and drove into DC for my meeting with

Jim at three o'clock. I met Jim's number one and two guys—Wells Griffith and Justin Clark. I knew Justin from him assisting us in Indiana, as he had been the Connecticut state director then. My stomachache got worse as the day went on. We discussed my role in the campaign going forward. Jim wanted me to continue overseeing the ground campaign in New Hampshire through the general election. We wrapped up and I headed for the airport, nearly doubling over in pain. I called Denise and told her that she might be taking me to the emergency room when I landed. At about twelve o'clock that night, I was diagnosed with pancreatitis. I spent the next four days in the hospital recovering and was good to go.

I was given the task of recruiting volunteers for the ground campaign into New Hampshire from Massachusetts, Connecticut, Vermont, Rhode Island, and New York. Before long, I was also connecting with other establishment groups from the South and as far away as California who had volunteers that wanted to fly in to help us out. It was inspiring to see so many people of every walk of life committing to this cause. Each state director was told to give me whatever I needed, and this was their number one priority. Even though New Hampshire only held four electoral votes, we thought they might be the most important votes to be had. The prediction was that it was going to be a very close race between Mr. Trump and Hillary Clinton. That's why Maine was left off the list of sending volunteers to New Hampshire. The thought was, even the one county in Maine tilting toward Mr. Trump was worth one electoral vote and that one vote could be the difference. As the RNC field team was being put together, I began contacting each state director and planning a strategy of how to pull in volunteers and then get them to New Hampshire. Another responsibility which came along with this was putting volunteers up in hotels and how we would feed them.

I took a day away from this on August 6 to drive in the motorcade again with Jason. Mr. Trump was coming to Cape Cod for a fundraiser and we needed to pick him up in Hyannis, Massachusetts. We suited up again, picked up our two black Suburbans, and headed for the Cape. We were like the dynamic duo and absolutely loved doing this together. Now we were driving for the president-elect, and security was tighter than ever. I knew everyone arriving with Mr. Trump by now, and again had current Treasury Secretary Steve Mnuchin sitting next to me. We left the airport and headed for Osterville. We were in Liberal land now and Main Street was lined with protesters. The staff in both of our vehicles rolled their windows down and waved to them all; it was pretty funny. As we got closer to the event location, the streets were lined with Trump supporters, and we tooted and waved. After the event I had to bring Steven and his fiancée to a particular hotel, then hooked up with Jason and headed back to New Hampshire.

As we headed into August, my days became longer and longer, but at least I was home. The good Lord had kept me safe to continue doing His work, and Denise was right by my side. On August 26, we attended the opening of a new Trump campaign office in Hudson, Massachusetts. It was here we met the new Massachusetts State Director, Vincent DeVito. This was a big deal and well attended. Radio host Howie Carr was there signing autographs and speaking as well. I went to look for DeVito to discuss some topics and he was nowhere to be found. He had left the event early which I found not only disappointing but disturbing. However, it was a clear sign of what was to come working with this guy. He was a part-time state director, although I'm sure the staff above thought he was working full time. He was one of my most disliked people I'd encounter through the entire campaign. I had worked with Trump state directors all over the country and they were incredibly dedicated. This was just the beginning, and the worst was yet to come.

Boston skyline from Logan International Airport
picking up Mr. Trump coming in for a fund raiser

CHAPTER 15

The Ground Campaign Continues and How the New Hampshire GOP Blew It

T he general election was gearing up and we needed the most experienced staff possible to be successful in the ground campaign and we got them. Jason was hired by the RNC to be a field coordinator, along with Charles Bruckerhoff and Alex Henry—one of our all-star volunteers who also showed up in many states to assist our ground game. Joe Forkin from the Ohio staff and my friend Aleks Urosevic from Wisconsin also arrived in New Hampshire. It was great to be working with these guys again, although this time they were not under my direct tutelage. They were paid by the RNC and reported to the command of the New Hampshire RNC, along with Trump State Director Matt Ciepielowski. As time went on, it became a struggle for all of them. Ultimately, the RNC controlled what was happening in New Hampshire. The leadership operated with good intentions and was very professional for the most part, except when it came to managing people.

They had a handful of their own field reps that were already part of the New Hampshire RNC. However, the handful of Trump staff who took positions as field reps had worked the ground campaign with me across many states. I always treated my guys with respect and never talked down to them. All of a sudden, they were being told what to do, how to do it, how high to jump, and not to ask questions. The RNC had this military mind-set which didn't sit well, and they were all coming to me for answers. Eventually, even a few of the RNC staff were calling me for help. Half of my life had been managing people in different capacities to accomplish different tasks. One main function which always provided success was treating your people the way you wanted to be treated. Don't ask them to do something you wouldn't do yourself. Be firm but fair with everyone. There were times through our travels across the country that someone would question my instructions and I would listen to what they had to say. If they had a better idea and it made sense, we did it that way. I allowed them to feel empowered, that their input was important which it was. Without them, I was nothing. With them and their one hundred percent commitment, we were a dynamic team. I had grown to love and respect nearly every one of them as they would do anything to accomplish our goals.

I had to make several calls to RNC State Director Ben Mitchell and his team to help them see the light, to help them see that treating people this way was not a recipe for success. Some would've quit if I had not intervened. As I mentioned, they were good people; they just weren't particularly great managers. Most times, they agreed with my perspective or ideas on how to do things differently and things improved as weeks went by, although my dear friend Charles was one who had enough and packed it up and went home to Connecticut. Charles was seventy years young, a veteran of the Army, and was not about to be treated with a lack of respect by *some snot-nosed little shit* from the RNC, as he put it. There was one particular instance where a young RNC staffer said to some volunteers upon going door knocking, "You two can work with the old guy," referring to Charles. When I heard this, I called Ben and lit him up. I didn't work for these guys, I worked for Mr. Trump and I'd be damned if I was going to tolerate any of them belittling my guys, especially someone who was as dedicated to the cause as Charles was from day one. Most of these RNC staffers were not Trump supporters until they were forced to be. To most of them, it was simply a job. To us, it was a mission to save America, and the only one with the stones to do it was Donald

J. Trump. So I said goodbye to my friend one last time. I hated to see him go as it hurt us due to his experience and energy level, but I respected his decision.

My number one priority was to funnel volunteers into New Hampshire, organize which part of the state to send them, and arrange dates and times they would organize with our field coordinators. I had to communicate directly with the volunteers to arrange arrival and departure dates, who they would be working with in the field, and then get back to them with all their hotel information and confirmations. Once I knew exactly when they were coming and going, I then relayed their information and the hotel I chose to the Trump travel team in New York. I also constantly communicated with several Trump state directors to get their lists of volunteers. I communicated with all of the field reps daily in order for things to go smoothly. It was back to fourteen to sixteen hours every day of the week. Denise would bring me lunch and dinner at my desk 90 percent of the time. I began to realize this was becoming a daunting task for one person. Right about this time, I was requested to put together a budget for what the ground campaign was going to cost in New Hampshire, something I didn't need to do when Mr. Trump was picking up the tab.

Shortly before this, Denise and I had bumped into Bonnie Johnson at the Massachusetts open house event in Hudson. Bonnie had been the Trump Massachusetts field director through the primary. She was a great person and a hard worker. When I realized I was going to need an assistant to help with our ground campaign in New Hampshire, I thought of her. She accepted my offer and was brought onboard and paid by the RNC but reported to me. She was worth every cent we paid her and was a tremendous help to me. Along with that, we worked very well together, and through this became good friends. She's a wonderful Christian and we always felt the good Lord brought us together. To this day, we always keep in touch as this created a wonderful bond. She was a tireless worker, and soon enough we would be tested more than either of us knew. Bonnie and I coordinated thousands of volunteers into New Hampshire, arranging hotels, rental vehicles, and tying them all into teams to work with a dozen field reps all over the state. At times, we coordinated twelve-passenger vans to drive to Boston and pick up Republican college students coming up to help on weekends.

One particularly trying time we had was when I had to coordinate dozens of people coming from Alabama and Missouri who were coming in for the last two weeks before election day. Some of them we even paid their airfare. They were arriving in small groups at different times and I had to arrange to pick them up at the airport and get them to their hotels. There were a few that were real yahoos. They were actually upset that we didn't rent them each their own rental vehicle. They were nice people but more of a pain in the ass than they were worth. I had made sure to inform all of them that it was quite a bit colder here than what they were used to, so bring layers for door knocking. Many of them griped about needing to go out with our field team and instead wanted to stay in and phone bank. One guy in particular informed us after he arrived that he had a special diet and expected us to accommodate him. Sorry, that's not the way it worked, so we politely informed him he'd need to buy his own food. We fed all of our volunteers during the election but it was fast food. He even went so far as to ask us to buy him a convection cooker of some sort for his hotel room. That was the last straw. We told him to pack up and made arrangements to get him to the airport and back to Missouri. Things seemed to improve with the rest of them after that.

Every Trump state director was extremely helpful, except one. Massachusetts State Director Vincent DeVito. In my opinion, I found him to be insincere, condescending, belligerent, and an all-around jerk to deal with, and that's being kind. DeVito was a Charlie Baker supporter. Baker is the current Massachusetts Governor who DeVito helped get into office. Charlie Baker was not a Trump supporter whatsoever. So Devito slipping into that role was simply a way for him to get to DC. He would tell anyone anything in order for them to do his bidding. I was told of several instances in which he'd have restaurant owners set up for a debate watch party, tell them he would take care of the expense, and then not bother to send in the necessary paperwork so they would be reimbursed. And there were a variety of similar instances. He created many stressful times for Bonnie and I by arbitrarily sending volunteers to New Hampshire without us knowing they were coming. He'd tell them to show up at different campaign offices and that we'd take care of their hotels.

Many times, we had irate people calling us who were stuck without a place to stay. We were often scrambling at eight o'clock or later on Friday or Saturday nights to find accommodations for volunteers. We were also attempting to organize buses of volunteers from Massachusetts and New York. Everything went off without a hitch in every state in terms of coordination, except with Massachusetts. With about two weeks to go before Election Day, DeVito sent out a mass email telling would-be volunteers that there will be a bus leaving Quincy, Massachusetts, that upcoming Friday night. The problem was it was Monday of the same week. Virtually impossible to organize the responses which came in over the next few days and confirm details with each person along with making hotel accommodations. Not to mention organizing with the field reps how and who they would need to pick up and work with at whatever particular field office. There was not a doubt in our minds that this was done deliberately. I made sure DeVito knew exactly what I thought of him and to the people above us as well. He was very coy in his response to anyone confronting him on issues and would act as though he didn't know what they were talking about. If I could've sent this guy to the moon, I would have. In my opinion, DeVito cost New Hampshire a lot of votes. We would have and should have had a lot more volunteers helping from Massachusetts. He was more of an obstruction rather than a resource.

Nevertheless, Bonnie and I worked day and night seven days a week calling volunteers, pulling them to New Hampshire, scheduling their times to assist, and coordinating with the field in order to get the maximum effort we could. Most helped our door knocking campaign but some came to do phone banking as well. It was a colossal effort and I never could have succeeded without Bonnie Johnson's assistance. Week after week, Jason and his teams turned in the highest door knocking numbers of any field rep in New Hampshire. I wasn't surprised since he was the hardest working and most seasoned leader out of them all. He had done it month after month, from the East Coast to the West Coast. We owed him a ton of gratitude and he deserved it. We went right up to Election Day and waited for the payoff.

The GOP was doing their own thing as well, and although they should've been supporting our presidential nominee, they didn't full-heartedly. The New Hampshire Republican Party, being led by state GOP chair Jennifer Horn, didn't help us any. I ran into Horn in the Nashua, New Hampshire, campaign office toward the end of the campaign. She came in with another woman, and they began telling people what to do. I confronted her, and someone stepped in to tell us to stop. If you didn't like Mr. Trump, you were not a friend of mine. Not in this realm, anyway. She came in there as though she ran the whole show. I found her to be a crass, nasty, and ignorant woman. To make things even worse for us, the GOP hired Ross Berry as Executive Director in June 2015. Neither of them were Trump supporters, and all you needed to do was walk into the GOP offices around the state to see it. Denise and I walked into the Keene campaign office one night and there was hardly a Trump sign to be found, although there were plenty of Senator Kelley Ayotte signs, as well as other New Hampshire officials running for office. Kelley Ayotte was off the Trump train, then on, then off again for good toward the end.

I was told by one of my best guys that Ross Berry sat in his Concord office most days playing solitaire on his laptop and telling people what to do. The office closet was full of cases of beer. It wasn't unusual to find empty beer bottles on Berry's desk among all the trash which was all over the floor as well. I was also told of many times when he did interact with volunteers who were there to help and that he was rude and belligerent to them. It was disgraceful that the state GOP leadership didn't have the capacity to see beyond its own shortsightedness. When history looks back at how New Hampshire lost in the presidential election to Hillary Clinton, by one percentage point I might add, an enormous part of the blame goes to Republican Senator Kelley Ayotte, Jennifer Horn, and Ross Berry. Ayotte lost her seat in the Senate in this election as well. Certainly not supporting Mr. Trump was a big part of that loss which would hurt us down the road.

Denise, Bonnie and I Sept 2016

Mr. Trump leased VP to be Mike Pence
his own plane. Manchester NH

CHAPTER 16

D-Day November 8 and Voter Fraud

P resident-elect Trump came to New Hampshire one last time the night of November 7, and one last time, Jason and I would drive staff vehicles in the motorcade. The protection from Secret Service, state police, and local police was very intense. Mr. Trump was coming to the SNU Arena which held 12,000 people and it was overflowing. Denise was inside texting me on what was happening and it was one of the few times that I wished I was inside rather than driving. Toward the end of the event, some of the staff came out before Mr. Trump and one was Political Director Michael Glassner. I hadn't seen Michael for months as he was assigned to travel with Vice President-elect Mike Pence. I walked over to Jason's Suburban as he was about to get in and said, "Michael." He turned, gave me a hug, and we chatted for a few minutes. It was good to see him. Michael was just one of those truly nice guys who always made you feel appreciated. One last time, Mr. Trump rocked them at a New Hampshire rally, and then we were off to the airport, blue lights blazing into the night.

I had arranged with Keith Schiller, Mr. Trump's bodyguard, to have a last one-on-one with Mr. Trump. The motorcade pulled up to the big Boeing 757 one last time. Keith was next to me, and as we came to a stop, he said "Okay, Sid. Let's go," and we trotted up to Mr. Trump. Keith hadn't told the Secret Service we were planning this and they were ready to draw their weapons. I walked up to Mr. Trump and said hello. I had Denise's hardcover of *The Art of the Deal* which she wanted me to get autographed, but this time to her. Mr. Trump asked me her name and began writing while at the same time asking me, "How are we looking here, Sid?" I told him what I felt was the truth. I replied, "We're going to pull it off, Mr. Trump, but it's going to be close." He thanked me for all I had done, shook my hand, and we said goodbye. I got behind the wheel of the Suburban and opened the book to see what Mr. Trump had written. Denise was going to kill me. He again wrote, *Dear Denise, best wishes. Donald Trump,* along with *You Have a Great Husband.* She wanted this one personalized to her, but I didn't feel comfortable telling the president-elect what to write. She was a little disappointed but again understood. Jason and I returned the SUVs and talked about what a great ride we had through the campaign. We talked about how incredibly blessed we were to have had this privilege. We gave each other a long hug and said goodbye, knowing we had one more day to go.

Election Day, at last. Everything we had worked a year and a half for would be decided in a matter of hours. We had poll sitters in several voting locations, as well as volunteers watching for voter fraud. There were situations of voter fraud being reported in one of the largest southern cities, Nashua. There were vehicles pulling up with Massachusetts license plates by the dozens. This was a typical routine in New Hampshire every four years. New Hampshire has some of the most relaxed voting laws in the country. You can come here from another state and vote without showing any identification. All you needed to do was fill out and sign an affidavit stating you were planning on moving to New Hampshire. If this isn't a recipe for voter fraud, I don't know what is. Hundreds, if not thousands, of liberals from Massachusetts would simply drive over the border, vote, and drive back. But, God forbid, you wear a Trump sweatshirt into your voting location. As I was standing in line to cast my vote, a gentleman came over to me and asked me to take off my sweatshirt. I proclaimed my outrage and was told it's the law. That's how ridiculously asinine the PC culture has become. I reluctantly took it off, and immediately upon entering the voting booth, put it back on. I opened the curtain, zipped it up, and very proudly and slowly walked out of the building, hoping to piss off any Liberal jackass who might be offended.

During the last week, Bonnie and I were asked by Matt to direct the efforts at the Nashua campaign office as it was being run by one of the RNC screwballs. The woman they had put in charge was clearly off-balance and the pressure had her melting down. We spent our day there until around 7:00 p.m. I headed for home to pick up Denise so we could attend a large party at a local country club with hundreds of supporters and staff. We were one of the few who never doubted for a second that we were going to win this. After all, we had God on our side. If you don't believe so, then you explain how anyone else could've pulled this off. Divine intervention was at work, and Denise and I believed so from the very beginning. We all gathered and watched the big screen with the results coming in. As the night went on, Mr. Trump gradually pulled further and further ahead. As more and more states fell to Mr. Trump, the room rocked with applause. Florida, Ohio, North Carolina, Wisconsin, and even Michigan went red. The election rolled on late into the night with Mr. Trump way ahead, but it still couldn't be called. Clinton's campaign chairman, John Podesta, came out and told their supporters to go home, telling them it would be decided tomorrow. I recall it sounding like the Wizard of Oz telling Dorothy to come back another day. The witch part certainly had some similarities anyway.

We left the venue at two o'clock in the morning, still not having a decision. Pennsylvania was still in the balance and would be the state to push Mr. Trump over the top. Jason, Denise, and I had driven together, and as we pulled into our driveway, it was announced on the radio the new forty-fifth President of the United States, Donald J. Trump! In fact, Pennsylvania was very close but tipped to Mr. Trump. The three of us were screaming in the driveway, hugging each other, and crying. These were the happiest tears I'd ever shed. It certainly gave me some idea of what athletes feel when they win a championship, something I'd never experienced. *We won!* Our country was saved for at least four more years anyway. The embarrassment of the Obama regime was over. The decimation of our military was over. The loss of millions of jobs and thousands of companies would soon be over. At last, we could feel proud to be an American again and we were confident President Trump would fulfill his campaign promises, unlike most of the politicians before him. It was three o'clock in the morning and my cell phone rang. It was my friend Ron Broadway from Texas. He called to congratulate and thank me for everything I had contributed to this wonderful night. I was so appreciative of Ron taking time to reach out to me. We'd never met but it felt like we'd known each other for years. Jason left, and Denise and I held each other and cried. The good Lord had blessed us again and cast his love upon us. We finally closed our eyes at 5:00 a.m. A new day had dawned.

My best pal and I after we won

Election night Never doubted we would not win

My best pal Jason and I at watch party night Nov 9th 2016.
We wouldn't know until almost 3am that we won

Nov 7th last trip to NH. Mr. Trump
signing Denise's Book for me

Nov 11th One last get together for many of the
team we traveled around the country with

CHAPTER 17

The Aftermath

How strange it seemed for it to be all over. November 9 was a day of euphoria. After all, the witch was dead. We were glued to the television, awaiting Hillary's concession speech. If not for Clinton, I might have felt bad. Watching the pain and anguish on her face was priceless. How could you feel bad for someone so nasty, so corrupt, and so arrogant? Hillary, Obama, and all the slimeballs in the media felt they had this in the bag. After all, they had done everything humanly possible to steal this election as they'd done so many times before. Ever hear of ACORN? Not this time, sweetheart. Our all mighty God had enough and was intent on saving our country despite what the devil herself had done to win—her husband, Slick Willy, meeting up with Attorney General Loretta Lynch privately in a personal jet for an hour. Sure, they were just trading family stories. It had nothing to do with making sure that the rat, FBI Director James Comey, didn't hang her out to dry and cost her the election. Right!

We found it hilarious reading about and watching the snowflakes on the news grappling with the thought of their new President. How pathetic and at the same time sad to watch so many of a generation have a meltdown over an election. This is what happens when you're raised in a culture growing up where everyone wins and there are no losers. Reality hits hard when you realize that there really are winners and losers, and not everyone gets a trophy. We felt embarrassed for them, watching them cry on television over this. And, of course, the left wing media and liberal loony tunes all have contributed to this degradation of our society. Protecting little Johnnie and Suzie from the world of reality, except for television. This loss had them reeling. Colleges offered therapy classes! Can you imagine? Tell me the socialist media isn't out to control the minds of our youth. Reality TV is where we watch degenerate after degenerate portray their television life as real.

Now their college tuitions won't be free, they're going to actually need to work hard to pay for them. Maybe protesting against how expensive tuition is would be a good idea. Perhaps cutting the ridiculous paychecks some of these Liberal ex-hippie college professors are making might be a good place to start. I have the solution to cure Progressive Liberals—send them to a country like Venezuela for a year to live in a socialist society, then see if they think capitalism is a better way of life. We marveled watching the media grapple with the results. How could this have possibly happened? Protests began all over the country. Profanity-laden comments by people who should've been arrested for saying things like "I'm thinking of blowing up the White House" as Madonna did. She starred in one of my favorite movies, Evita. She played the role of an intelligent, very classy first lady, Argentine political leader Eva Peron. What a shame she fell so far from what she could have been as she's turned out to be nothing like the character she played.

The devil is alive and is everywhere. Just look at our ex-President, Lucifer himself. Barry Soetoro a.k.a. Barack Hussein Obama. Barry wasn't born in the United States. He was born in Mombasa, Kenya, on August 4, 1961, according to an affidavit of Reverend Kweli Shuhubia. Kenyan officials with the Provincial Civil Registrar state there were records of Ann Durham, his mother, giving birth to little Barry in Mombasa, Kenya, on that date. His grandmother in Kenya gave an interview in October 2008, and was adamant that she was present during his birth in Kenya. Obama was destined by the devil to take down this God-loving country, the United States of America. This country was founded on Christianity and the belief in God. Look at what's been happening for the past several decades. Gradually, the progressive liberal left has been attempting to take God out of our society. Think that's just a coincidence? Think again. Obama did everything in his power to break down American society as we know it. Do you think President Trump would ever socialize with a homegrown terrorist like Bill Ayers? The silence was deafening.

Ayer's was the founder of the Weather Underground, a self-described communist revolutionary group in the 1960s. They conducted a campaign of bombing public buildings, including police stations, the US Capitol building, and the Pentagon. He was a college professor in Chicago for years later in life, teaching our youth. He made more than one visit to the White House during Obama's tenure. Does this not tell you something about Obama's character? After all, birds of a feather flock together, as they say. But now the Lord has stepped in and said enough is enough. He knew it would take someone like Donald J. Trump to pull enough people together to stop the evil people who have been running this country into the ground. There was no other candidate who could have or would have stood up to what President Trump was put through and continues to be put through. If President Trump did half the things Obama and Hillary had done, the left wing media would have his head. Why don't they? Because it's a rigged game, that's why. *Drain the swamp* wasn't just a campaign slogan; it's a metaphor for what President Trump is truly up against. Middle class Americans voiced their feelings on November 8, 2016. Enough was enough.

Walter Cronkite must be rolling over in his grave watching what the hacks in today's liberal media were doing to fuel the division in the country. Like a bunch of spoiled brats, some college students began rioting in and around their schools. They didn't get their way, and burning cars and buildings was their immature way of showing their displeasure. Protest marches were set up in cities around the country, paid for by the Dems and George Soros. The fake news media covered it all, justifying it the whole time and rarely denouncing the violence. Many of the heads of these media organizations contributed megabucks to the Clinton campaign and they were pissed off that all their money went to waste. As we all know, negative news sells better than good news, and when you are motivated by greed and power, how can you be impartial? You can't, and hence we have the fall of respectable journalism in this country. Completely biased journalists and reporters who no longer report the facts but instead input their own feelings and bias into their reporting. We best all pray that God continues to bless America and the evil of socialism doesn't take a foothold in this great country of ours.

CHAPTER 18

The Waiting Game Ends

I t was time to move on, the campaign was over, and I needed to find a job. Come to find out, I would be on a list to get a job as a political appointee. There wasn't any specific timeframe other than sometime within a few months. My problem was, I couldn't look for a career job knowing I'd be heading to DC within a couple of months. So I took a job driving for an airport service in order to make ends meet. Not exactly a dream job as many mornings I was up at three o'clock for 4:00 a.m. pickups. In order to find a job suitable in the administration, Trump staff was instructed to review what's called the Plum Book. The Plum Book holds all of the staff positions available in the White House and all of the government offices in Washington, along with pay scales. We were instructed to submit three options of jobs we thought would be a good fit. This is the part I never gave much thought to—what I'd like to do as a political appointee. My choices were Department of Agriculture, Department of Energy, or Department of Transportation. I didn't have experience in any of those areas but I had a wealth of managerial experience. I was confident I could apply that and the interpersonal skills I had developed in sales and find a suitable fit somewhere that I could serve my country well.

This is where I began to see the side of politics I didn't care for. I was realizing that it wasn't what you knew but who you knew that got you ahead of others. I had made a few enemies over the course of the campaign. People I had called out for not giving it their all or people I felt were there for self-serving reasons. As it turned out, a couple of these people were on one of the committees that decided who got what and where. Shortly after the election, there were groups of staff people who were called to Trump Tower in New York to begin organizing this effort. Another weasel who made this list was Louisiana State Director Ryan Lambert. Lambert was another self-serving individual who also had *little man syndrome.* Toward the end of our efforts in New Hampshire in the general election, he was flown in to help us out. You would've thought the King of England had arrived to save the day. This is the same guy who would park his rental car directly in front of the door at the campaign office in Nebraska rather than leave that space for a volunteer. We tangled toward the end of the campaign because he didn't have a clue what he was doing, and made Bonnie's and my job much more difficult than it needed to be.

I'm sure when these knuckleheads saw my name come up, in all likelihood, they pushed me further down the line. December came and went without a phone call from anyone in New York or DC. Matt Ciepielowski received a call and had a position. Then I began to hear of others receiving calls that had half of the responsibility and tenure I had during the campaign. Denise and I received our tickets for the inauguration but weren't sure if we would attend. Denise's daughter Meaghan was expecting a baby right around the twentieth of January, something we wanted to be home for. We prayed that I'd get a call or something good would happen. About mid-January, I began making a few phone calls to people I knew in DC from the campaign. Delaware State Director Joe Uddo was one, and Wells Griffith was the other. Wells was Deputy Field Director under Jim Murphy. Every government office in DC has liaisons to the White House and was responsible for filling political appointee positions. These guys were in the Department of Energy and filled that role. I remember Joe saying, "Sid, you deserve to be here as much as anyone after all you did." He got the ball rolling, and we agreed on a pay level and a start date—February 20, 2017.

Our prayers had been answered and Denise and I were thrilled. I'd be serving my country and still working for now President Trump. We planned that I would drive down to DC on February 19 and would be staying in Bethesda, Maryland. My good friend from the campaign, Robert Bowes, was allowing me to stay in his rental home for two weeks while I looked for a more permanent place. There was one slight hiccup but it didn't keep me from going to DC. On February 11. I was working for the airport service and driving two customers to Derry, New Hampshire. It was snowing pretty hard as I came onto the highway. The traffic was fairly heavy, and I was attempting to merge when *wham!* We were rear-ended by a young male driver who admitted that he was going to pass me. He must have decided at the last minute that was a bad choice, but by this time he was going way too fast and couldn't stop. I had instant pain in the middle of my back and also my neck. Both passengers in the back were thrown forward into the seats.

I was put onto a stretcher and taken away to the hospital. My passengers were not hurt, and another car was sent to get them. After several hours, X-rays, and a CAT scan, I was sent home with medications and told to rest. Fortunately, there was nothing broken. It was all muscle damage. Over the next several days, Denise took care of me as the pain got worse as the week went on—typical symptoms of this type of accident, I was told. Nevertheless, I had to go to DC on the nineteenth, as we needed this job. I felt well enough to leave and packed up the car on the eighteenth. The morning of Sunday the nineteenth, Denise and I prayed for a safe journey and thanked the Lord for our good fortune and blessings. Our goal was for her to move to DC with me within a few months. Leaving and saying goodbye to each other was very difficult. We had become closer than at any time since we met, but we knew this would mean a better future for us. I was leaving my sweetheart home alone, again. But this was a path the Lord had set, and we were at peace with that.

CHAPTER 19

My New Position as Political Appointee

M onday, February 20 was a holiday so this gave me time to figure out the transit system in the area. On Tuesday the twenty-first, I took a bus to the Bethesda subway terminal and was fortunate to get some help from a few nice people finding my way into DC. It was a very confusing place for someone who's not used to traveling on public transportation. I came up from the subway station in DC to the hustle and bustle of the nerve center for the entire United States. I would soon learn that nearly every decision made in these buildings has an impact on the life of all Americans. I was in awe, and thought to myself, *Pinch me.* I'm actually working in Washington, DC. for the federal government. After languishing in the public transportation confusion for a week, I decided to buy a parking pass and drive in and out of DC. There I was, driving past the Jefferson and Washington Memorials on my way to work, it was incredibly beautiful. If you had told me ten years ago this is where I'd be, I would've laughed and said you were crazy. It was real, and I was proud as hell to have made it this far, so were Denise and my family. If only my father had survived a couple more years, he, too, would have been proud of his oldest son.

My first introduction upon entering the Department of Energy building was getting set up with a security badge. You could not get in or out of the building without it. There were multiple armed guards at every doorway. Finding my way to the seventh floor was like walking through a maze. The building was split in half, with walkways going from one to the other and every floor looked identical. With a little help, I found my way up to Joe Uddo's office which was in the Secretary's end of the building. There was an armed guard at this entrance and you needed to wave your security badge over the electronic door opener to get access. We stopped at Wells Griffith's office so I could say hello and thanked him for all he did to get me there. I hadn't seen him since last August 2016. We talked about which internal department might be a good fit and also where they still needed some eyes and ears. What I came to find out was all of the political appointees, and there were about thirty of us, were there to learn and watch what the existing personnel were doing from day to day, making sure the new agenda of President Trump was being followed.

After eight years of the Obama regime, there were a lot of Liberals in this building and most of them hated President Trump. Their world order was turned upside down, and there were going to be extreme policy changes which they didn't agree with. While discussing their strategy of which internal department to install me, Joe mentioned to have me shadow with Suzie Jaworowski. My dear friend Suzie, Indiana State Director who I worked so closely with during the primary was here in the Department of Energy. I was thrilled and couldn't wait to see her. Joe then brought me to the Department of Technology Transitions and introduced me to a few of the staff. The DOE, Department of Energy, is comprised of many departments relative to every energy source you can think of. There's oil, electricity, wind, fossil fuel, nuclear, and others. Each department has a Director and a support staff, many being scientists, geologists, and contractors. Technology Transitions works directly with the seventeen national laboratories across the country and their scientists. Its function is to maximize the capabilities of the labs and accelerate the transfer of research to commercialization. The national laboratories give the Unites States an undeniable strategic advantage in the global marketplace.

I was introduced to Don MacDonald, Senior Advisor for Strategic Projects. Don had been in the DOE for twenty-four years and was a wealth of knowledge and a great guy. Halfway through my meeting, my cell phone rang. It was Suzie wanting to know where I was. She came into the office of OTT and knocked on the door. I opened the door, and we just hugged each other. The good Lord had brought us together again and we were both so happy to see each other. Suzie was one of the best and most dedicated people I'd met on the campaign trail. She was simply a child of God and an absolutely wonderful person all around, and we had bonded in a special way in the relatively short time we worked together in Indiana. Neither of us thought we'd have this opportunity again. We arranged to meet later that day and discuss how best to work me into the daily regimen. I continued my meeting with Don as he explained the history of the national labs and their function. It was fascinating and intriguing, not to mention invaluable as I would soon find myself planted in OTT.

I continued commuting from Bethesda, Maryland, into DC each day. My friend Robert Bowes, whose house I was staying at was able to give me another week there, although I needed to find another residence pretty quickly. As I've found the Lord often does, He put another person in my life at a necessary and helpful time—Elias Rella. Elias was a Trump staffer from New Hampshire and had been working at the Department of Agriculture since January 19, 2017. We had worked together during the presidential primary, although Elias lived and worked in Northern New Hampshire so we didn't see a lot of each other. Denise was actually closer to Elias than me due to her taking over the Keene campaign office. Elias and I hooked up on the phone one day while I was in DC. He needed to move out from where he was staying and was looking for a roommate. Earlier when he had moved to DC, he rented a room from a homeowner not too far from the Department of Agriculture. What he didn't know until it was too late, the homeowner was a devout Liberal and hated Trump. Elias had to move. No sooner had we begun discussing it when a fellow worker offered him to rent a room in her house. As it turned out, she had two rooms to rent. Apparently, this is a very common thing to do when you live in the DC area due to the transient nature of the political field.

Amanda Lockwood would become my new landlord, as well as a very good friend. The downside to this was she lived in Fredericksburg, Virginia. Without traffic, an hour ride into DC. With traffic, morning and night, two and a half hours commuting each way, it was horrible. Leave the house at 5:30 a.m., arrive in DC at 8:00 a.m. Leave DC at night around 5:30 p.m. and get home about 8:00 p.m. To make it even worse, the drivers down there are the rudest and most obnoxious drivers I've encountered in the entire country, and I've been to most states during my life. They made Bostonians seem like Amish people on the road! It made me long for home. Elias was a twenty-year-old young man and a good Christian. He was also the most mature, kindest, and trustworthy twenty-year-old I think I've ever met. I moved into Amanda's at the end of my second week in DC. While living there, I also learned about slugs. Strange, I had always thought the term only applied to a slimy type of earth crawler and a handful of people I had worked with through the campaign. I soon realized this is also a term used for commuters in the DC area. A slug is someone who parks their vehicle at a Park & Ride, and then gets picked up by a complete stranger for their commute into DC.

In the DC metro area, which consists of DC, Maryland, and Virginia, you cannot use the HOV lanes without a minimum of three people in your vehicle. Therefore, if you choose to be a *slug*, you commute for free. The benefit to the person who picks up is that they get to pay a lesser toll amount and get into DC quicker by using the HOV lanes. And there are actually rules for slugs found online; for example, you're not supposed to strike up a conversation unless the driver chooses to. It's one of the strangest things I've ever heard of, but then again, DC is a strange place. So I began this grind without much choice, but my days were filled with learning new things. Basically, you went from meeting to meeting of your choice in several different departments. For example, I was involved in two meetings with a company by the name of NuScale, talking about the benefit of SMRs, Small Modular Reactors. Advanced SMRs offer many advantages, such as a relatively small size, reduced capital investment, ability to be sited in locations not possible for larger nuclear plants, and provisions for incremental power additions. SMRs also offer distinct safeguards, security, and nonproliferation advantages. NuScale was presenting their case in promoting SMRs which I believe is clearly a good direction for the US to be going in. The US has a few older nuclear reactors which will be taken offline soon.

I was introduced to the acting Director of OTT, Rochelle Blaustein. Rochelle is one of the most accomplished people I've ever had the good fortune to meet. We had several meetings about the mission of OTT and the role I could play. We both felt one missing component in OTT was someone who could sell the mission of OTT to the private commercialized business sector in order to successfully bring our labs and commercialization together to provide extremely new innovations to help humanity. Rochelle introduced me to Sanjiv Malhotra, Director of the Clean Energy Investment Center and part of OTT. Sanjiv and I had three or four meetings discussing how we could best work together and utilize my skill set in professional sales, management, team and relationship building. I moved into an office in OTT on the seventh floor of the Department of Energy with Rochelle's blessing. In private, she had expressed that she wanted me to apply for the role of Director of Technology Transitions and she would support me. We both felt I was the missing link this department needed. The pay scale was about $150,000 a year as Director, and I was up for the challenge.

On March 6, I got to meet my new boss, Department of Energy Secretary Rick Perry. I was in the auditorium in DOE when Secretary Perry gave his speech to all of us. I was thirty feet away from him and it was an honor. I met him and his wife at the end of his introduction speech, and they were very sincere and down-to-earth people. This was getting more exciting by the day, and I loved my role serving my country and now President Trump. At this point, I had pretty much stopped shadowing Suzie and was entrenching myself into OTT. On Tuesday the seventh of March, I was introduced by Rochelle to the rest of the OTT staff who were on the fifth floor. I was introduced as a political appointee and that I was now working primarily in this department. I could sense that some of the staff wasn't all that excited to meet me. They were all in place from the Obama Administration; a few I could tell were *snowflakes*. Rochelle explained to them that I was going to be working with them but did not describe my exact role. However, from conversations I'd begun to have with people in other departments, the word was beginning to get around that I may be looking at the role of Director of OTT.

CHAPTER 20

A Rush to Judgment

The evening of March 9, I received a strange email. It was from the Editor-in-Chief of Greentech Media, Stephen Lacey. I'd never heard of this man before and he was asking if I could call him. He'd like to talk with me about something interesting he'd seen. I had no idea what he was talking about. Following the same protocol which we followed during the campaign, I wasn't talking to the media about anything. We didn't trust them for one split second. They most often twisted and manipulated words in order to fulfill their agenda. We watched the media try to skewer President Trump from June 2015, right to this very day and it wasn't going to happen to me. I mentioned it to Elias and Amada that night, and we all shrugged our shoulders. I thought I'd simply ignore him and he'd go away. On March 10 at about 10:00 a.m., I received another email from Lacey into my DOE mailbox. This time, he mentioned that he found what I had written in my Twitter *to be very interesting coming from a political appointee.* Lacey offered to hear my side before he went live with the story. I felt like I was stuck between a rock and hard place. I emailed him back, referring him to the DOE's Public Affairs office.

I was left wondering what in the heck this guy could be talking about. I hadn't touched my Twitter account for as long as I could remember. As a matter of fact, I assumed it was closed since I hadn't used it for so long. How wrong I was and figured I'd better see what this guy was talking about. When I opened it, there it was—my last tweet from early December 2015. It was shortly after the shootings in San Bernardino, California. At the time, Mr. Trump had posted the picture of the couple who were involved in the killings. I was angry about it, just like millions of other Americans. This was the third murder or attempted murder by Muslim jihadists in recent months, and now it was happening on our own turf again. I was never a big social media person and opened my Twitter account shortly before this horrible event. I felt like putting in my two cents' for what it was worth. Under the picture of the couple, I wrote *scum sucking maggots, exterminate them all*. What I was referring to was any other Muslim jihadists who would kill innocent people in the name of religion. My mother has been married to a Turkish gentleman for twenty-five years. Our entire family loves him as he's a terrific person, and more importantly, treats my mother like gold. I was not calling for the extermination of all Muslims.

I had a sick feeling in the pit of my stomach as I could sense what was coming and I wasn't wrong. I walked down the hall to the Public Affairs office and told them what was happening and went back to my office. At approximately 11:30 a.m., Joe Uddo called me and asked me what was going on. He had received a call from Public Affairs telling him what was happening with this potentially explosive story. I explained the series of emails and the threat to go live with the story from Greentech Media. I headed down to Joe's office and met with him and Wells Griffith. They explained that this could potentially cost me my job if this story received a lot of traction and depending on how the media twisted it. They understood what I said was innocent but that it could easily be misperceived and twisted around. They had to make some phone calls and suggested I go back to my office and wait to hear from them. An hour later, Joe called me and requested my presence in his office. The story had hit online and every news group was rewriting it and putting it out in their online media with their own spin. Within thirty minutes, Politico, BuzzFeed, NBC News, Washington Post, NewsMax, and dozens of other online media news feeds went live with the story. It got the traction of studded snow tires on ice.

Every one of them in their headline twisted my words to interpret me wanting the extermination of all Muslims. It was like a pool of sharks being tossed a live fish, as they went into a feeding frenzy. Joe looked at me, and with great frustration in his face, told me they had called over to the White House looking for direction on how to best handle this. The response back was I am to be terminated or I could resign. I sat there for what felt like an eternity—stunned— as I grappled with the reality of what was happening. This had to be a nightmare. I also understood that this would reflect poorly on President Trump's administration, so I told him and Wells that I would go back to my office and write a resignation letter. I've never felt so dejected in my entire life. It felt as though my whole world was collapsing around me. I felt numb as I stood up and headed back to my office. There, I wrote, *I, Sidney Bowdidge, hereby resign from my position in the Department of Energy as of this day.* I packed up my DOE issued laptop and cell phone, and went back to see Joe and Wells. I felt bad for them as I knew this was difficult for them to do. They both knew how much I had given to the campaign and they were upset that someone had done this to me and that they had to be the ones to cut me loose.

Joe walked me to the elevator, telling me that everything would be okay. I leaned against the elevator wall, dejected, listening to him. I could see this bothered him deeply. The door began to close and I couldn't help letting a tear run down my cheek as I gave him a last wave and thanked him for everything. Crushed would be an understatement. That morning, I had driven into DC in my car with Amanda and Elias. Right after I wrote my resignation letter, I texted them both, letting them know that I just resigned. Naturally, they were confused and at first thought it was a joke until I reaffirmed that it wasn't. They both told their superiors that an emergency came up and they needed to leave early. As I came out of the parking garage under the DOE building, they were both waiting on the corner for me. Amanda got in the passenger's side and asked if I was okay. I've always been a sensitive guy and not one to hold in my emotions. I was angry that someone would do something like this to me, but also disappointed in myself. Denise was so proud of me. We had come so far together and our future was looking so bright. With all these emotions going on, I began to cry. It was that upsetting.

Amanda got out and came around to my door, opening it and telling me that she would drive us. She hugged me and was crying herself. She and Elias were extremely angry and upset. It's truly amazing how politics on one hand can be such a nasty business, but on another, can bond people together as I'd never experienced before. I told them what had gone down and they wanted to know who had done it. Obviously, someone in the department had called Stephen Lacey at Greentech Media. I would find out this was *the* publication and source of information for what was going on when it came to anything and everything in the energy world. I then made one of the most difficult phone calls I've ever made—I called Denise. She was shocked and naturally upset and furious. Who would want to do this and why? She said a prayer for us and pointed out that this is not what the Lord wanted, that's for sure. This was the devil's work and we knew it had to be some progressive Liberal working in my department. I recalled how I had attended a meeting with the entire staff in OTT a few days earlier, and we calculated it was probably one of them.

On our drive back to Fredericksburg, I began getting calls and text messages from friends and colleagues asking me what happened. By the time we got home, Denise called with the discovery of the perpetrator. The original article in GTM pointed out how a certain Teryn Norris, an ex-DOE/OTT employee under the Obama administration called this in. I suspect he was friends with others in OTT who must've reached out to him. He did the legwork into my social media background and he was quite proud of himself in the article, backed up by his Facebook post. It was cruel and disturbing, and my reaction was anger. I wanted revenge. This was character assassination at its best, all with the purpose of hurting someone. Shortly after we arrived back in Fredericksburg, Denise and I spoke again, only a much different conversation than earlier. We both were very hurt and angry, but she pointed out how the Lord would want us to forgive this guy. Through my entire life, I had lived *an eye for an eye.* You hurt me and I'll hurt you even more. But I knew she was right.

This anger would eat me up if I held onto it and I'd be giving in to the devil's work.

As a Christian, I knew I had to forgive. It's what God wants and it's the right thing to do. By forgiving him, I free myself from the debilitating anger which would linger. Denise and I prayed for this guy, and we prayed for the Lord to help us forgive him. I felt such a relief after we did this. Sure, I had forgiven people since I began my relationship with God, but forgiveness for doing something like this? But I did, and it helped me focus on positive energy toward what I was going to do going forward. We prayed for the Lord to show us a direction, and in time, He did just that. I was at peace with our decision and I now began reaching out to people in DC where I might find another opportunity. I called Trump ex-campaign manager Corey Lewandowski. Corey hadn't heard yet and he was shocked but not surprised. He felt terrible this had happened. He certainly knew best of anyone what I had contributed but also was aware of the dynamics of the swamp. There probably wasn't much he could do but said he'd try. I then called Michael Glassner who today is the Executive Director at Donald J. Trump for President. Michael explained to me that this type of instance unfortunately *leaves you toxic.*

Through the course of two days, news article upon news article rewrote the story, each putting their own twist on it. They all made me out to be a completely incompetent massage therapist who had no business working in DOE. None of them looked further into who I was. There were other articles on Google from my past, such as being selected to the President's Club for Hunter Engineering where I was always a top sales rep. Clearly that wouldn't fit into their narrative to make the Trump administration look as inept as possible. First, they expounded on the original article stating I was a massage therapist. That information came from the interview with Lifezette back in June 2015. In that interview, Denise and I were asked what we did for a living. I pointed out that my background was in sales, marketing, and management, but I just recently was delving into massage therapy. As I previously pointed out, that article *only* mentioned me being a massage therapist. During that time, I posted an ad on Backpage.com looking for business. There are many legitimate ads on Backpage but, of course, the media made out that what I was doing had some form of illegitimacy to it. Once Denise and I became wrapped up in the Trump campaign, I had completely dropped what I was doing. We were onto bigger and better things, such as helping to save our country. Even though Stephen Lacey was the catalyst for what happened, I don't fault him. He was doing his job. Once I returned home, he actually took the time to interview me over the phone. The next day, he wrote another article on me, this time in a more positive light. It's currently the first article which comes up when you look up my name on Google. I deeply appreciated him doing this as he didn't need to.

I stayed in DC for a few weeks in hopes of finding another opportunity. During this time, I finally met my friend Ron Broadway. I had reached out to Ron and discovered he had opened an office in DC relative to his business. He wanted to discuss the possibility of hiring me to run it, if he was going to move ahead. We met at the new Trump International Hotel on Pennsylvania Avenue. We'd never met but had talked on the phone many times throughout the campaign. Ron was always helping us in whatever way he could and called many times during my travels across the country, just to see how we were doing. We talked about what had happened to me, as well as my background. We discussed his new office and the direction he was looking to go, along with how I would fit into his plan. We concluded our meeting and I left, walking back to my car which I had parked at the Department of Agriculture building. It was cold and windy. The previous night had dropped about four inches of snow in the DC area. The city was shut down and nearly empty. This was good fortune for me, as my normal commute of two and a half hours was just over an hour each way.

I stayed at Amanda's in Fredericksburg for a few weeks after my departure from DOE. Some nights I prepared dinner for Amanda and Elias after their long days. We'd sit at the table for hours talking over cocktails about our lives and this whole adventure. Amanda was a die-hard Trump supporter, so we always had plenty to talk about. It became apparent that nothing was going to transpire anytime soon, anyway. It was time to go home. Denise and I hadn't seen each other for several weeks and we were missing each other terribly. The bond we now had was awesome, thanks to the guidance of the Lord. He brought me to Him through her and then set us on a path which would create a deep love and trust, experiencing an adventure most people don't get to experience. From the night I watched *God's Not Dead*, I never once wavered from my newfound belief in our Lord. The love of new friends continued right to the end. Toward the end of March, I packed up and prepared to leave Fredericksburg at four in the morning for my several hours' drive home. I had bought some flowers for Amanda to show my gratitude for all she had done. Then I left this goodbye note to my new dear friends:

> Dear Amanda and Elias,
>
> Thank you for being there for me during one of the most difficult times in my life. I'm forever grateful for your friendship. In my prayers this morning, the Lord helped me see what this entire experience was truly about—the love of God in which we all reside. It wasn't about a job or how much money I could make. It was about the love of good friends to which I found in you. I love you both and may God bless you.
>
> Love,
> Sid

AFTERWORD

I have many times asked myself, what is my purpose in this life? Are we here just to survive? Are we here to make as much money as possible and live a comfortable life? Are we here to have nice cars and toys? Or are we here to make a difference in this crazy world? I've never felt such a level of fulfillment as I have since June 2015. From the day the Holy Spirit came to me, my life changed for the better. It became easy for me to love unconditionally. It became easy for me to forgive and have more compassion and understanding. That's what a difference walking with God in your heart can make. Without any doubt in my mind, God intervened in this election. I believe Liberals would laugh and scoff at that comment because most live a godless life, just as I used to. This wonderful country was born and founded on the belief in God. Progressive Liberals are, and have been for decades, tearing apart the moral fabric of this country. The influence from movies, television, and the delusional left wing media has left millions without a moral compass.

Do you believe that you have a soul? I do. Do you believe that our bodies, our flesh simply functions without a soul, something to drive it? I believe we have a soul, and if we believe in Jesus and give our lives to Him, there will be life after death, just as it says in scripture. Our flesh gets old and dies but not our soul. If you believe in God, then you believe in good. If God represents good, then I also believe that Satan represents evil. How else would you explain the horrible things that we see in our lives and throughout history? If you have yet to listen to Paul Harvey's *If I were the Devil* on YouTube, you should! Very few, if anyone else, could have pulled off what President

Trump did. The Liberal media refuses to acknowledge anything good that he's done and he's accomplished a lot to make this country great again. Sure, he's unorthodox, but that's what got him there. From the first day Denise and I saw him speak in Bedford, New Hampshire, we believed in his message and his sincerity to be President. We'd watched for decades as our country was being dismantled piece by piece. Now it's time to put it back together.

Short of President Ronald Reagan, nearly every President before and after him in the Industrial Age contributed to weakening the United States. With the advent of television and cinema, the cancer seeds of socialism were spread. President Trump is spot on when he talks about fake news. The heads of most of these outlets are devout progressive Liberals who understand how to twist information and know if they tell people the same thing long enough many will believe it as truth. Communist Russia communicated their propaganda via art, literature, and cinema. Obviously, there was no internet, otherwise this would have been used as well. Joseph Stalin used his propaganda machine to rule Russia for decades. The concept of *socialism in one country* became a central tenet of Soviet society. During his time as Russian leader, millions of so-called *enemies of the working class,* including senior political and military figures were interned in prison camps, exiled, or executed. Eventually, his autocratic government oversaw mass repressions, thousands of executions, and millions of deaths through famines and labor camps. Hitler's propaganda machine was even more attuned to brainwashing the public, and look what happened there.

The PC culture has been dismantling Christian society as we know it for decades. Their supporting American Civil Liberties Union is nothing more than the driving force behind creating a society where God does not exist. Run by progressive liberal lawyers, none of these people want balance; they want power and nothing more. Yet they portray themselves as protecting people's rights. When in reality, all they want is to take away the rights of the populace. If the Clinton machine had won, without question our Second Amendment would have been taken away. The sick people who walk into a school and open fire are just that—sick people. They should be locked up in a mental institution but we don't have mental institutions any longer. Why, you might ask? Because it's no longer politically correct to label someone as disturbed or mentally ill. Most of the mental institutions have been closed across the country thanks to the PC culture. And now the burden is put on our hospitals that can't begin to absorb the quantity of mentally ill people walking around in our society. The answer has become to medicate these people. And when they don't take their meds, the results sometimes become lethal. Taking guns away from law abiding citizens is not the answer. Don't agree? Look at France and you need look no further.

I could write a book on what progressive Liberals are doing to this country to destroy it but I'm sure there are many. Liberals see life through rainbow-colored glasses. They're narrow-minded and typically only care about their point of view. As I write this, our First Amendment of free speech is under attack from our own colleges, no less. Obama doubled down and pushed this train to even higher speeds over his eight long years. I'm confident he's quite proud of his hand in creating what was becoming a Socialist America. But God's not going to allow that to happen. America is His shining star of what is good on this planet. We're not perfect but we are the best of what's here. President Trump's not perfect but he's the perfect man for the job at this time in history. I was never able to serve my country in the military due to my hand injury at seventeen, but I did get to serve my country in a different sense. I was able to help save my country from the scourge of socialism and I'm damn proud of it. You see, God had a plan for me and I followed it. The Lord worked through Denise in order to get me to do something I'd never done before. She knew she was being called to help; that's the way she's always been. I knew she was right. We had to help, even if it was simply making phone calls for the campaign.

The more they said we couldn't do it the more determined we became to do more. When asked to run the ground campaign across the country, I knew I had to step up just as I had in New Hampshire. I got to experience the love of God across the heartland of America. I made lifelong friendships along the way and worked with wonderful people all across the country, all for a common cause. Thank God for the volunteers for whom without we wouldn't have won—thousands of God-loving people, Trump-loving people who contributed hours and hours of their time for free. To all of you, thank you from the bottom of my heart. The missed birthdays and holidays as we traveled from New Hampshire to California, it was all worth it and I'd do it again in a heartbeat. Thank you to Denise who never doubted me and was behind me all the way. Thank you to my best friend Jason Squeglia for being beside me through the entire ride. You are an incredible man. Thank you to President Donald J. Trump and his family for putting themselves through the dissention they are going through from the Left. Most importantly, let's be grateful to our Lord and Savior Jesus Christ for placing an army in front of the evil of socialism.

So the next time someone says to you "Hey, let's go volunteer," do it. You never know what you can do until you try. You never know what God's plan might be unless you're listening.

Today, I'm self-employed as an independent sales rep selling mobile marketing. Denise's mother had a massive stroke shortly after I returned home from DC. Since then, she quit her job and helps care for her mother. We joined a church new to us in our town of Bedford and attend regularly. I find being involved in a church helps keep me feeling closer to God. We've found new friends—people much like us who love, who forgive, who pray, and just care more about others. It's God's way. Things haven't been easy, but through our faith, things never seem insurmountable. God has continued to put people in our lives unexpectedly who have helped us through some struggles—Christians like us. People ask me if I'll get involved in the next presidential election. To this point, I have little interest. There's no duplicating what we did and how we did it. I was blessed to be part of the most historic run for President in our history. That being said, if that's where God chooses for me to be again, who am I to say no? After everything that happened, we are nothing but grateful to our Father for all that we have been given. We find happiness from many of the small things in life. I'm not the same person I was before June 2015, and friends and family notice it. God changed my heart; He filled me with the Holy Spirit. I'm happier than I've ever been and more at peace with myself and who I am. I am a believer.

My best friend Jason Squeglia and I talk nearly every day and see each other frequently. He went back to running his environmental business in Massachusetts. Jason and I are closer than brothers and I'm so grateful for his friendship. My dear friend Charles Bruckerhoff is turning seventy and still has the energy of a forty-year-old. Charles went back to his semi-retirement life in Connecticut but we stay in touch frequently as well. Robert Bowes has a great position in DC and deserves everything good that comes his way. Many of my other friends and associates are currently employed in different agencies in Washington DC. We all were called by the good Lord above to help save America and to help make America great again. I'm so proud of all of these guys and grateful for their sacrifice, grateful for their friendship, and grateful for their belief in me to lead them across the country in accomplishing what everyone said couldn't be done.

Shortly after I returned from DC, several people said to me that I should write a book about my journey. It was something I hadn't considered, but God planted the seed. I prayed over it and asked the Lord if this is what He wanted me to do. I've found that if you listen to your heart, that's where God puts His answer. I felt it and He told me why. It would be inspirational to others. It may help others to do something they've never done before. It may inspire people to come to the Lord, to discover what it's like to be born again. Perhaps even nonbelievers just like me will become believers, too. It's a peacefulness you just don't know until you're there with Him. I didn't write this book to make money, although if it does, much of it will go to our church, our children, charities, and others who need help. I was blessed to have taken the journey of a lifetime. I hope you enjoyed it as well.

May God bless you and may God bless America!

ABOUT THE AUTHOR

Sid Bowdidge is a God-loving, hard-working loving father from New Hampshire. He's had a long and successful career in sales and management and never passes up a challenge to excel in life. Part of his success has been having a; *glass is half full* positive attitude. The love of God has changed who he was in many ways for the better. Now a spiritual man, who put his country before himself for what he believed was right. Most of the photos within this book, were taken by the author.

CPSIA information can be obtained
at www.ICGtesting.com
Printed in the USA
LVHW011450100521
687001LV00004B/154